D0742423

THE EARLY LIFE OF SEAN O'CASEY

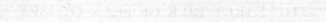

MARTIN B. MARGULIES

THE EARLY LIFE OF
SEAN O'CASEY

THE DOLMEN PRESS

TO MY PARENTS

Set in Caslon type, and
printed and published in the Republic of Ireland at
the Dolmen Press, 8 Herbert Place, Dublin 2

1970

Distributed outside Ireland, except in the U.S.A.
and in Canada by Oxford University Press
and in the U.S.A. and in Canada
by Dufour Editions Inc.,
Chester Springs, Pennsylvania, 19425.

SBN 19 647543 0

INTRODUCTION

When I came to Dublin in the fall of 1964, it was to undertake a postgraduate course of study in legal history at University College, not to write about Sean O'Casey. But I never did earn my degree, at least not in Dublin. What happened was simple. Admiration for O'Casey and his works had been one of the factors which lured me to Ireland. About midway through the academic year, I became bored with my dissertation. So instead of secluding myself in the National Library, I began to visit some of O'Casey's neighborhoods, speak to his surviving friends and relatives, and hunt for records. Invariably each informant directed me to another, and each new document suggested further avenues of inquiry, until I discovered that in just three or four months' time I had accumulated an immense store of information, much of it hitherto unknown, and some of it inconsistent with the prevailing image of O'Casey as a product of the Dublin slums. But my investigation had been unsystematic, to say the least, and it was not until it was nearly over that it occurred to me to write a book. By that time, I was ready to leave Ireland, and it was too late to retrace my footsteps.

This accounts for the absence of footnotes in the text. It explains, also, some serious shortcomings, chief of which is the absence of any mention of O'Casey's early writings. Fortunately this subject has been treated with thoroughness in Robert Hogan's *Feathers From the Green Crow*. I offer the book to the public nevertheless because I think it contains valuable information about O'Casey's early life and standard of living, and reconstructs his childhood and young manhood as completely as possible given the paucity of surviving witnesses and documents. Dublin is still a city of cohesive neighborhoods, and therefore I think I was able to interview just about every living Dubliner who had had significant contacts with the young O'Casey or his family. Most had never been approached before; many can never be approached again, as nearly all were in their seventies or eighties, and not a few are now deceased. I am a lawyer by profession, and have been a journalist, so I know full well how unreliable testimonial information can be. I have tried to use my training to check carefully the authenticity of what I was told. In addition, I have been singularly fortunate in tracking down pertinent photographs, records, and documents, thanks largely to the generous cooperation of various Irish civil servants and O'Casey's friends and relatives, many of whom have become personal friends of mine. They are too numerous to acknowledge by name, but I must mention the Beaver family — Alicia, Harry, Maureen and Lorraine — and their aunt, the late Mrs. Isabella Beaver Murphy, whose homes were always open to me. I wish also to thank Prof. David Krause, O'Casey's friend and biographer, who was kind enough figuratively to tear my early manuscripts to pieces until I had finally turned out a publishable product. Thanks, too, to Gabriel Fallon and Prof. Ben Collins of the University of North Dakota, who read and criticized the text, and to my father and Miss Dymphna

6

Devlin, who accompanied me around Dublin taking photographs of major sites.

In lieu of footnotes, I shall set forth in this introduction my principal sources of information. I interviewed fifty-six people, including ten of O'Casey's relatives, seventeen of his former neighbors, two of his superiors on the Great Northern Railway, three of his comrades in the Irish Republican Brotherhood, six fellow-Irish Citizen Army members, ten of his friends at the Laurence O'Toole's club, and six drinking companions of his inimitable brother Mick. Two of my informants don't fall into any category: journalist R. M. Fox and William Middleton, son of O'Casey's old friend George Middleton, but their contributions were valuable nevertheless. Information about births and marriages came from records at St. Mary's Church and the Custom House. School records of O'Casey's brothers were found at the Central Model Schools on Marlboro Street. O'Casey's own school records were snatched from a wastebasket in St. Mary's National School the day before the building was placed on auction sale. I have since turned them over to the authorities at St. Mary's Church. His sister Bella's school records are in the custody of the Department of Education, though I warn the student that he will have a weary time trying to find them. Thom's Directory and the Valuation Office at 9 Ely Place provided much of the data about the valuation, rent, and dates of occupancy of O'Casey's houses (the latter corroborated in many cases by addresses on birth, marriage, and death certificates.) I scrutinized

7

the records at Mount Jerome cemetery, where most of the Caseys are interred, and of Nicholl's funeral home, which handled the burial arrangements. From the Society for Irish Church Missions I learned the salary and dates of employment of O'Casey's father. The British Army Record Office supplied me with all available data — unfortunately incomplete — about the military careers of Mick and Tom. Documents pertaining to Bella's teaching career are available at the Public Records Office. General information about military salary scales came from the British Ministry of Defence, and about Post Office salary scales from the Irish Department of Posts and Telegraphs. Information about living conditions in Dublin was garnered largely from the Report of the Dublin Housing Commission, issued in the wake of the transport strike of 1913. In no instance have I relied for a single fact on O'Casey's autobiographies, except where noted in the text.

THE EARLY LIFE OF SEAN O'CASEY

The antecedents and early life of Sean O'Casey are shrouded in mystery which six volumes of autobiography do not dispel. As one commentator has remarked, the autobiographies tell us a great deal about what O'Casey thought and felt, but very little about what he actually did. Names are changed, dates are rarely given, descriptions of locations are vague. When he gets specific we are no better off, because he is often wrong. Perhaps he took artistic liberties with his material; perhaps on occasion his memory simply failed him. Whatever the reason, the autobiographies are not historical records. To do their author justice, they were never intended to be.

The real records — the grammar school rollbooks, the registries of births, marriages, and deaths — are somewhat more productive of concrete information. But serious gaps remain. The lower middle classes of a metropolis leave few traces behind them. Much of the data which was once available perished in the fires of Easter Week and the war of independence which followed. Some was lost through neglect. The records from St. Mary's National School, where O'Casey studied for three years, were rescued from a wastebasket, rat-eaten but still legible, as the building in which they were housed was being cleaned before going on the auction block. However, the rolls of St. Barnabas', where O'Casey also went to school for several months, have simply disappeared.

Many Dubliners survive who knew O'Casey as a fairly young man, but only one who knew him when he was a boy. And such eyewitness testimony is fraught with pitfalls. The informants were reporting things which they had seen, or perhaps heard from others, more than fifty years ago. Some of their statements were clearly self-serving. And even honest recollections can be tainted by bias, self-justification, and self-aggrandizement — as O'Casey's sometimes was.

As a result, there is much about the young O'Casey which can only be guessed at, and still more which will never emerge wholly from the shadows. Yet there are enough hard facts scattered here and there around Dublin to enable us — with the aid of some cautious speculation — to sketch in outline O'Casey's early years.

O'Casey's real name was John Casey. At times he called himself John O'Casey, and at other times Sean O Cathasaigh, and he finally settled on Sean O'Casey when he began writing for the stage. His father, Michael Casey, was the lone Protestant offspring of a mixed marriage, and was raised on a farm in Kerry or Limerick, depending on which of his descendants one chooses to believe. By 1863, when he was 26 or 27, he had come to Dublin, where he lived at 22 Chamber Street, near the Coombe. The house has long since been demolished, but if it resembled its neighbors it was a shabby brick building, two stories in height with a shop on the ground floor, and dirty grey in the manner of so many Dublin houses whose original colors have withered under several generations' onslaught of damp air and soot. It stood on the south side of Dublin, not far from Swift's St. Patrick's, in the heart of the Liberties, which had been the center of a bustling silk trade less than a century before. In recent years the entire section had fallen into decay and was now — according to a contemporary English tourist guide — shunned by visitors on account of its desolation.

We first encounter Michael in 1863, when he married a Protestant girl named Susan Archer, who lived on the same street. We can only guess at their ages, since their birth certificates are not available and the age on the burial certificates are often inaccurate, but it would seem from the latter that both were in their late twenties, and Susan was slightly older than her husband. Moreover, her antecedents were better, for whereas his father had been a farmer, hers was an auctioneer, and a fairly prosperous one too, if family tradition can be credited. Otherwise we know little about him, except that he had at least two other daughters, Elizabeth and Isabella. The Christian names of the Archers are instructive in themselves. None is common in Ireland, and all bear witness to the family's Anglo-Protestant origins.

The marriage took place on January 27, in St. Catherine's Church in Thomas Street. In front of that church sixty years earlier Robert Emmet had launched his hopeless uprising, and paid for his folly on a temporary gallows. Half a century later, the Caseys' youngest son would play a modest role in the inception of another rebellion, which appeared at the time to be equally foolhardy and futile.

II

Though both Caseys were Protestant, neither was born into the Protestant garrison, that select band of Anglo-Irish who constituted almost a separate nation within Ireland, alien in religion and even in race to the Irish Catholic masses whom they ruled. However, any Protestant could identify with them, especially if he were a communicant of the established Church of Ireland. In caste-conscious Dublin, whose inhabitants are full of the snobbery of the dispossessed, this identification enabled the Protestant to feel socially and morally superior to his Catholic neighbors, and hold up his head in times of economic adversity.

The Caseys in 1863 required no such anchor to respectability. Financially, Michael was doing tolerably well. His marriage certificate discloses that he was working as a clerk at the time of the wedding, a position which not only paid a relatively comfortable salary but conferred upon its holder a measure of social status. The following November, he began to moonlight as an assistant teacher at the Night School run by the Society for Church Missions, where he earned fifteen shillings a month. Then, within a very few weeks, he went to work for the Mission full time as an assistant clerk in its central office. There, in a dingy building on Townsend Street in the shadow of Trinity College, he toiled nearly a quarter century for five pounds, fifteen shillings and eight pence a month. The salary, though hardly princely, amounted to approximately twice what the Dublin manual laborer could expect to earn. And it wasn't only the salary which drew Michael to the Mission. The society was a proselytizing agency, whose members were imbued with the dour zeal of militant Protestantism. For Michael, fervently devout, the position represented not merely a livelihood but a calling.

The young couple moved often during the first few years of their marriage, no doubt in response to actual or anticipated increases in the size of their family. Their first recorded move took them across the Liffey to 22 Wellington Street, but thereafter they remained in the same general neighborhood, in the manner of many lower and lower middle class Dubliners who live out their lives within a block or two of their birthplace. The first two Casey children to survive to maturity were born at 22 Wellington Street: Isabella Charlotte (the 'Ella' of the autobiographies) on February 6, 1865, and Michael Harding ('Mick') on the last day of 1866. But when Tom was born on February 2, 1869, the Caseys were living at $23\frac{1}{2}$ Dorset Street; they were at 57 Wellington Street when the first of three infants named John was born — and died — two years later; and at 6 Upper Dorset for the birth of Isaac Archer ('Archie') in November, 1873. Of these houses, only 22 Wellington still stands, a two-storied, whitewalled building on the corner of Upper Dorset Street, with an ornate Georgian doorway and a shop on the ground floor. Since the others were all within hailing distance of it, it is reasonable to conclude that all partook of the cheerless respectability common to the entire neighborhood. Judging from available evidence — the condition of the surrounding area, the appearance of 22 Wellington Street, Michael's in-

13

come — it is unlikely that any of them was a slum.

The neighborhood school, St. Mary's, was part of the Irish national school system — secular in theory, highly sectarian in practise, and governed by a Commission whose regulations enjoined its teachers to inculcate 'the duties of respect to superiors, and obedience to all persons placed in authority'. The function of such a system was not to educate, but to teach the working-class Irish their place. So, when his children reached school age, Michael Casey enrolled them instead in the Central Model Schools in Marlboro Street. These also were run by the Commission, but here the teachers were better paid and more carefully selected, and the pupils were charged modest fees. Most were the children of aspiring middle class parents who could not afford private education. A retired civil servant named George Carr Shaw sent his son, George Bernard, to the Model Schools.

In those days of casual and non-compulsory attendance, the three Casey boys rarely missed a day of classes, though the truancy rate was high among their schoolmates. But they were poor students. Michael and Tom failed several subjects, doubtless from want of application rather than low intelligence. Their father is said to have obtained private tutoring for them from the headmaster himself, in consequence of which they not only received their certificates, or diplomas, but are reported to have served as assistant teachers and trained, briefly, for teaching careers. Isaac, whose family remembers him as a mathematical wizard and who spent most of his adult life as a clerk, showed early promise by flunking arithmetic and bookkeeping. Isaac was less fortunate than his brothers, for his father died before his final year. There was no private tutoring for him, and no certificate either.

Bella alone applied herself. She graduated with honors in four of her five senior subjects, receiving as a special prize three beautifully bound volumes of Shakespeare. Two survive; Mick pawned the third when he was thirsty. In 1882 she entered the Teachers' Training College, also on Marlboro Street, to embark on a two-year course which would qualify her for appointment as a Principal Teacher.

Meanwhile, in 1879, the Caseys had moved again, this time to 85 Upper Dorset Street, on the corner of White's Lane. 85 Upper Dorset has long since given way to a bank, but its description can be inferred from its tax valuation of twenty pounds. This figure, according to present-day Dublin housing officials, suggests a three or four story building, in good condition, with a minimum of seven or eight rooms. Such a building hardly qualifies as a slum. Nor was it a tenement. 'Tenement' and 'slum' are not synonymous. 'Tenement' in Dublin is a legal term for a dwelling which meets two requirements: it accommodates two families or more, and its 'rates' — that is, the assessments for municipal services — are paid by the landlord rather than the tenants. Thom's Directory of Dublin householders for the year 1880 lists an 85 Upper Dorset Street, owned by Mr. William Lattimer. The sole listed tenant, and sole rate payer, was Michael Casey.

From this information one might conclude that Michael Casey occupied the entire premises alone. But even a Dublin clerk with a comfortable income and four children neither required nor could have afforded to lease a sprawling apartment building. A plausible explanation was volunteered in a letter from O'Casey's friend and biographer David Krause, whose information came from O'Casey himself. Michael Casey, according to Krause, merely managed the house for the landlord and rented out some of the rooms. This makes sense. The cost of putting four children through fee-charging schools had no doubt put a sizeable dent in his clerk's income; he would have welcomed the chance to perform part-time duties in return for a reduced rental. Yet a few questions remain to tantalize the curious. Why, for example, was Michael Casey paying the rates, and not William Lattimer, the landlord? And it is interesting that the sole listed ratepayer at Number 86 next door — also owned by Lattimer — was a Mr. McCrum, whose wife Elizabeth was Susan Casey's sister. Was he, too, serving as caretaker? And — if so — had he apprised his brother-in-law of a similar opening on the adjacent property?

One would like to know more about the big house on Dorset Street. For there, on March 30, 1880, Sean O'Casey was born. His mother's sister Isabella assisted at the birth, and made her mark in lieu of her signature on the birth certificate at the Customs House. On July 28, the infant was baptized in St. Mary's Church by the Rev. T. R. S. Collins, who later appears in the autobiographies as part of the composite figure whom O'Casey calls the Rev. T. R. S. Hunter. His parents christened him John. It was the name of his paternal grandfather, and of his two baby brothers who had died.

Irish politics in 1880 were moving slowly toward a dramatic climax which was yet a generation away, a climax in which the infant would play a significant part. Full eighty years had gone by since the Protestant Parliament in Dublin, frightened by peasant uprisings, had ratified the Act of Union and thus put an end to two decades of quasi-independence. During the first half of the succeeding century, Irish militants had agitated for repeal of the Penal Laws which reduced Irish Catholics to second class citizenship. This objective achieved, they were turning to other goals: scrapping the Act of Union in favor of some new, though as yet undefined relationship; and restoring to the peasants the land which the English invader had snatched from their ancestors. Both struggles were waged at two levels: on the legislative level, by the Irish Parliamentary Party, which generally held the balance of power between the two major parties, and under Parnell's direction was learning how to use it; on the popular level, by various associations, some open, some secret; some peaceful, some violent. At their core the two issues were one. Both grew out of the fact that there remained after seven centuries a militant minority of Irishmen who were not reconciled to the English conquest.

17

And in England, in the great gloomy building on the Thames where Irish destinies were fashioned by strangers, William Ewart Gladstone, newly triumphant over Beaconsfield and the Conservatives, was preparing to attack the Irish problem with two new laws: a land reform measure which alienated the English without placating the Irish, and a Coercion Bill which enraged the Irish without appeasing the English. Angry, brooding men of the Irish Republican Brotherhood, otherwise known as the Fenians, were muttering that the time was past for talk of Parliaments, except an Irish Parliament, sitting in the old Parliament House at College Green. But there hadn't been an Irish Parliament for eighty years. The old Parliament House was now the Bank of Ireland; the temple was given over to the money-changers.

The members of the Protestant garrison, whose ancestors had dominated that Parliament, had little reason to miss it. Their forbears had exchanged legislative autonomy for English protection against the masses who would have overwhelmed them. Slowly this protection was being eroded by reformers in England itself: men who spoke of electoral reform, land reform, home rule. But the day of reckoning was far in the future. For the present, the garrison appeared firm and enduring as ever, like the stones of Trinity College where its sons learned to rule.

Dublin was in decline in 1880. The city's economy, based formerly on the manufacture of silk and poplin, had fallen off badly since the Union, and two recent international exhibitions had failed to revive it. The population, too, was declining: from 255,000 in 1861 it had dropped to 245,000 ten years later. The once gay capital of an almost independent nation had lost its glitter with the passing of power to Westminster. The wealthy still turned out for the Dublin season, but many of the gracious town houses had fallen into decrepitude, and were leased as tenements. Their exteriors were handsome, their doorways adorned with ornate Georgian brass knockers, but within whole families huddled, four to six to a room, under ceilings painted by Italian masters. One building in twenty-five was uninhabited.

We cannot ignore this other Dublin, the Dublin of overflowing Georgian tenements and ramshackle hovels hidden in alley-ways behind tall houses. It was not the Dublin of O'Casey's family. But it was the Dublin with which he himself chose to identify from his early manhood.

In 1881 or 1882, the Caseys moved to 9 Innisfallen Parade. It is not difficult to guess the reason. Bella was living at the Marlboro Street Training College, where she was studying for her teaching certificate. With their only daughter gone, the family required less space.

Once again, they had moved scarcely the length of a stone's throw. Innisfallen Parade is a little avenue off the foot of Drumcondra Road, which is an extension of Dorset Street north of the North Circular Road. However, their new home bore no resemblance to the old. Innisfallen Parade consists of squat, red-bricked cottages, most of them only a single story high Number 9 contained a kitchen, a small bedroom in the back for Michael and Susan, and a large sitting room in the front where the boys probably slept. There was no indoor plumbing, but the Caseys had their own water tap and privy in the back yard, instead of having to share these amenities with a dozen or more neighbors in the manner of the Dublin poor. The houses were structurally sturdy. No tall buildings surrounded them to block out light and air. Living quarters were crowded, but there was none of the soul-destroying absence of privacy characteristic of the Dublin slums. The weekly rental for Number 9, six shillings six pence, was substantially more than the average weekly rent which working class families paid.

Mick and Tom, meanwhile, had drifted into civil service jobs at the Post Office: Mick, because he lacked the ambition to become an architect or teacher, as his father had hoped he would; Tom, because all his life he slavishly emulated Mick. Mick, by all accounts, was a talented youngster. He could sign his name with both hands simultaneously, and a surviving drawing shows him to have been a sensitive and accomplished artist. But he possessed none of the drives or enthusiasms which later fired his younger brother. He appears in a photograph, taken while he was in his early twenties, as a jaunty young bulldog of a fellow, well-groomed and nattily dressed. Mick was a hedonist, and the Civil Service supplied him with the means to indulge himself.

Post Office records for the period are sketchy and incomplete. There is no way to learn with certainty what duties the Casey brothers discharged, or what salaries they recieved. But Mick was probably working as a telegraphist and Tom as a letter-carrier, positions which they are known to have held some years afterward. And it is possible to deduce their incomes from the then-prevailing Post Office salary scales. These scales indicate that each boy was earning as much as his father, and with annual increments would soon earn considerably more.

Bella was a more successful scholar than her brothers. She was not admitted to the special class for gifted students, but she did better than average work in all her subjects and graduated in 1884. She performed poorly only in the keeping of her practise lesson-books, a chore which she evidently found mundane and tedious. St. Mary's had just opened an Infants' School in the basement of the large schoolhouse at 20 Lower Dominick Street. In February 1885, Bella was hired as its first Principal Teacher.

For twenty-seven pounds and ten shillings per annum, plus free lodging and 'results fees'— emoluments based on the number of pupils who passed their examinations, which were administered by inspectors from the Commission — Bella taught classes of thirty to fifty-seven infants and first-graders. There was a shortage of desks, and for a long time the school possessed no piano, but the young woman evidently overcame these obstacles. Her superiors were well satisfied with her performance. In their reports they commended her for her gentleness of manner and her skill in maintaining discipline, although one inspector suggested that she allow two recreation periods daily instead of one, while another saw little purpose in her teaching geography to infants. He advised Bella to discontinue the subject 'in favor of some better employment, say, sewing for the girls'. And Bella never did learn to keep her lesson books properly. The inspectors chided her repeatedly over mistakes in the records, and today the rat-eaten rollbooks still bear the corrections which she made at their insistence. Also, she appeared to lack ambition. She received a routine promotion at the end of her first year, but she never took an examination for further promotion, although free to do so at any time. Nor did she ever receive any of the gratuities or premiums which were sometimes awarded for outstanding service.

By 1885, Sean O'Casey was old enough to go to school. Already, however, he was suffering from the eye disease which would torment him for most of his life. Perhaps the father saw no point in lavishing money on the education of a youngster who might never be well enough to read. Or he may have feared that the boy would not be able to fend for himself at the Model Schools. At St. Mary's, there was Bella to look after him. So, in May 1885 O'Casey enrolled in the Infants' Class, and for nearly four years, Bella was his teacher.

Thus it is clear that O'Casey had more formal

education than he acknowledged in the autobiographies. In fact, the events in *I Knock at the Door* took place, not at St. Mary's but at St. Barnabas', which he attended briefly some years afterward. One may question, however, whether the condition of his eyes permitted him to derive much benefit from Bella's tutelage. Krause, who discussed the matter with O'Casey, told the writer in a letter that O'Casey went through St. Mary's without really learning how to read. Instead, his mother and sister read him long passages from the Bible and school primers at home. Then, when he was examined in school by the inspector, his extraordinary memory enabled him to recite these passages by rote, leading the examiner to believe that he was actually reading them.

Whether or not this is correct, O'Casey somehow contrived to pass all three of his annual examinations in reading, two of them with honors. Then he moved up to the first grade, where he added three new subjects: writing, math and spelling. He did honors work in all, except spelling, in which he received a 'Mere Pass.' Meanwhile he was also attending Sunday School, where in 1887 he received an illuminated scroll, second class, 'for proficiency in Holy Scripture and Church Formularies' on a diocesan examination. According to Krause, he earned this award in the same manner that he passed his examinations: by repeating from memory the passages he was supposed to be reading. In contrast to his brothers, his attendance record was spotty. During his first year he missed nearly half his classes, doubtless because of illness. But his health improved as he grew older, and during his last two years he was present most of the time.

By the time O'Casey progressed into the first grade, his father was no longer there. In January, 1886, Michael Casey had fallen ill. The disease, which O'Casey tells us arose out of an injury at work, affected the spine, leaving him bedridden and partially paralyzed. There was no workmen's compensation in those days, but his employers voted him a gratuity of seventeen pounds ten shillings — the equivalent of three months' salary — in recognition of his long period of service. He lingered through the summer, and then, on September 6, he died at the early age of forty-nine. He was interred at Mt. Jerome cemetery, at what was then the southern extremity of the city, and Bella was granted five days' leave from school to attend the funeral.

There couldn't have been much money left over after the medical and funeral expenses were paid. In fact, Michael Casey's estate was never admitted to probate, which suggests that it contained scarcely anything at all. Alive, the father had supported a large family comfortably on a modest income. It would be astonishing if he'd contrived to put any of it into savings, or leave his next of kin with anything more substantial than the bitter memory of a more prosperous period in their lives.

Mick and Tom also were gone. In October, 1887, each had left the Post Office and enlisted in the army: Tom in the Royal Dublin Fusiliers, and Mick in the Royal Engineers, where he worked as a tele-

24

graphist just as he had done as a civilian. Their
enlistment dealt another blow to Susan Casey's
pocketbook, for the Queen was not nearly so generous with her troops as with her civil servants. And,
considering the sort of woman that she was, it must
have dealt an even more crippling blow to her pride.
Irish private soldiers in the British Army were more
often working-class Catholics than educated Protest-
ants with white-collar jobs. Any uncertainty about
Susan Casey's opinion of common soldiers was dis-
pelled two years later, when her daughter married
one.

Bella met her husband through Mick and Tom.
Nicholas Beaver (the 'Benson' of the autobiographies)
was a professional soldier, the son of a color sergeant. Born in Co. Waterford, he'd entered the army
at fifteen as a drummer in the first company of the
King's Liverpools, where he'd risen to the rank of
lance corporal. Somehow he'd struck up a close
friendship with the Casey boys, and was probably
instrumental in inducing them to enlist. A photograph taken at about the time of the wedding shows
him, at 22, to have been strikingly handsome, with
dark hair and medium build, though his discharge
papers record that his left forearm and hand were
marred by tattooes. He was two years younger than
Bella, who was herself a beautiful young woman.
And he was Protestant, which was important. But he
was also a soldier.

O'Casey tells us that his mother didn't attend the
wedding, and this is credible enough: she also boy-
cotted the weddings of Tom and Isaac. Bella's two

25

daughters recall how, years afterward, when Beaver was dead and Bella desperately poor, their grandmother rebuked her often for having married against her wishes. If Bella had listened to her mother, Bella would not have spent her last years scrubbing other people's floors. Her mother never forgot it, and never permitted Bella to forget it either.

The marriage took place on March 7, 1889, at St. Mary's Church where the family worshipped. Shortly after the ceremony the newlyweds had to part, Bella to finish out the year at school, and Beaver to return to the South Aldershot Military Camp in England, where his twelve-year enlistment still had five years to run.

There is evidence that the family was hard-pressed even while Bella was working. In May, 1888, Isaac had left school and gone to work as an office boy for the Daily Express. Also, O'Casey told Krause that the family had moved from Innisfallen Parade — probably toward the close of the 1880s — and lived for a time with Bella on the top floor of 20 Dominick Street. Then, when Bella resigned from her job to bear her first child, Susan Casey had to manage on the income of the fifteen-year-old Isaac, together with whatever contributions her two oldest sons and her son-in-law were making out of their meager army paychecks.

But the Caseys were still far from poverty. In 1889, they moved from Dominick Street into a small but pleasant cottage at 25 Hawthorne Terrace. It had a tiny yard in the front, and a somewhat larger yard in the rear, the latter containing a water tap and dry privy for the exclusive use of the family. (A neighbor has confirmed O'Casey's account of how the sanitation men came once a month to carry off the contents of the privy in huge baskets, which they emptied into waiting carts, leaving a stench which clung to the walls for days afterward.) Indoors were two rooms and a kitchen. Both the tax valuation and the weekly rent were lower than at Innisfallen Parade: respectively seven pounds instead of nine, and six shillings instead of six shillings and six pence.

The family had changed neighborhoods as well as living quarters. Innisfallen Parade, Dorset Street, and Dominick Street were all fairly central, but Hawthorne Terrace was a quiet street in the northeast corner of Dublin. The area was populated by ships' captains, bottle blowers, and mechanics, most of whom were employed in factories which stood nearby. There were few, if any, tradesmen or unskilled factory workers. Years afterward, a man who grew up on Hawthorne Street in the 1880s and 1890s described his neighbors as lower middle class people, living in modest, bare comfort.

A new neighborhood meant a new school for Sean O'Casey. A few blocks away, across the Great Northern Railway tracks, stood St. Barnabas' Church. Like St. Mary's, it was Church of Ireland — still known in those days as the Established Church, though it had been disestablished for more than twenty years; again like St. Mary's, it supported a national school, located directly in back of the church building. Here O'Casey had a brief and final fling at formal education.

In *I Knock At the Door*, O'Casey devotes several chapters to his schooling. At least one reporter, Anthony Butler, has concluded that the events he described took place at St. Mary's. There is some skimpy evidence for this assertion. Massey and Ecret, for example, were classmates of O'Casey at St. Mary's, and the clergyman-school manager whom O'Casey calls 'Rev. T. R. S. Hunter', would appear at first to be the real-life Rev. T. R. S. Collins. But Collins supplied only the name. The personality almost certainly belonged to Rev. J. S. Fletcher of St. Barnabas', whose identity O'Casey probably disguised to avoid wounding his son, Rev. Harry Fletcher, whom the playwright deeply admired. And other evidence establishes conclusively that the incidents occurred at St. Barnabas', if indeed they occurred at all. George Middleton, for example, lived a block away from the Caseys and attended St. Barnabas' church and school for many years. Brady's Lane, where he fought the bullies, is around the corner from St. Barnabas. Today it is called Irvine Terrace. O'Casey's description of his wild flight home after he'd struck the schoolmaster with the latter's own ruler tallies precisely with the St. Barnabas neighborhood. And the schoolmaster himself, Schoolmaster Slogan of the autobiographies, was really John Hogan — a short, stocky, balding, middle-aged, hard-drinking native Irish speaker from Galway, whose students paid tribute to his strictness as a disciplinarian and his readiness with a cane by nicknaming him 'Bosch.'

We shall never know, however, whether O'Casey actually belted Hogan with a ruler. There is some circumstantial evidence that he did not. George Rocliffe, two classes behind O'Casey in the small schoolhouse, would surely have heard of so sensational an occurrence. But Rocliffe, who remembered Hogan vividly, knew nothing about it.

Rocliffe is the only person to describe O'Casey in early boyhood, other than O'Casey himself. The description is necessarily sketchy: Rocliffe was two years O'Casey's junior, and the youngsters had little to do with one another. However, Rocliffe remembers that O'Casey missed many classes, and, when he was present, his eyes were frequently bandaged. This led his classmates to tease him, but O'Casey won their respect by his eagerness to participate in their games in spite of his handicap. A determined youngster, he was not an aggressive one, never to Rocliffe's knowledge getting into a fight. All the pupils at St. Barnabas' seemed to Rocliffe well-fed and comfortably clad. Except for his bandaged eyes, O'Casey did not stand out in appearance from the others.

Beaver was discharged from the army in 1893. Armed with a letter from his commanding officer, describing him as 'honest, steady and sober', he obtained employment as a porter with the Great Northern Railway, and moved with his wife and baby daughter into a two-story cottage on Rutland Street, just off the North Circular Road. There they enjoyed the luxury, for that period, of indoor running water. The following year, Mick and Tom were back home, having been transferred to the inactive reserves. Both re-applied successfully for their old Post Office jobs, with Mick borrowing Bella's wristwatch to take the civil service examination, and pawning it afterward to help finance a celebration. Mick spent almost as many nights on Rutland Street as on Hawthorne Terrace. He would toss pebbles against the window and beg his sister for the use of her parlor couch when he was too drunk to face his mother.

There is no reason to believe that the family was in straitened circumstances during the mid-1890s. Hawthorne Terrace was not over-crowded by the standards of the day. There was a piano in the sitting room, a legacy from some former tenant. In that sitting room, Isaac — theater-struck long before his younger brother — constructed a stage, on which the neighborhood children acted out plays. According to Bella's eldest daughter, there were parts for everyone, including even the family mongrel. And there is one other piece of evidence from which we can deduce the Caseys' living standard. Thy took a number of studio photographs, which were not cheap in those days. There are at least two apiece of Mick and Tom, and one each of Bella, Susan, Nicholas Beaver, and Sean O'Casey, the latter taken when he was about twelve years old. All appear well-dressed and well-nourished.

While Bella had lived at Hawthorne Terrace, she had tutored O'Casey informally, using regular school texts. When she moved to Rutland Street the instruction came to a virtual halt, not so much because of the separation — the houses were no great distance from one another — as because O'Casey was approaching his fourteenth birthday, when Dublin boys customarily left school and went to work. We have nothing but O'Casey's own account of his working experiences, in which dates are not supplied and names are altered — fortunately, only slightly. The firm of 'Hymdim-Leadem', for example, can only have been the well-known Dublin chandlers' company of Hamptom-Leedom, on Henry Street, owned by the Deverell brothers, whom O'Casey called Dovergull. If O'Casey truly began working at the age of fourteen — which seems likely enough — he was hired in 1894. But that is all that we shall ever know, for the building was burnt during the Easter Rising of 1916, and the company's records destroyed. 'Jason's', where he worked for barely a week after leaving Hampton-Leedom, would have been Eason's, the leading Dublin news-dealer. O'Casey gives us a clue to the date when he tells us he obtained the position through the good offices of the Rev. Harry Fletcher. Fletcher came to the parish in 1896, so O'Casey would have worked for Eason's in 1896 or 1897.

Fletcher, still in his twenties, had come from Trinity College to serve St. Barnabas' as curate during the illness of his father, J. S. Fletcher. The old man had been somewhat a fundamentalist, but the son was a high churchman, who tried to brighten the severe Anglican ritual with some of the panoply of the Roman mass. Two hundred years after the battles of the Boyne and Aughrim, the more conservative members of his congregation still believed

31

that such practises bordered not only on heresy but on treason. Resplendent in their regalia of the Loyal Orange Order, and led by a police inspector and a railway foreman, they dominated the vestry and drove Fletcher from his pulpit and indeed from the country, only to be expelled from office themselves during the incumbency of his successor. The vestry minute-books contain no record of the struggle, but O'Casey's own account of it is readily confirmed by surviving parishioners.

Fletcher's tenure was brief, but his influence on O'Casey was profound. The youngster responded enthusaistically to the beauty of the high church ritual which Fletcher attempted to introduce. He submitted to confirmation, and for years afterward remained a zealous communicant. He is said to have taught Sunday School, and it is certain that when he first became interested in nationalism, he campaigned strenuously to have high church services rendered into Irish.

In 1897, Susan Casey moved for the last time. She and her four boys now occupied a two-room flat on the top floor of what is today Number 18 Abercorn Road, a greying, nondescript two-story building which lay literally in the shadow of St. Barnabas' Church. Across the street in front were the tracks of the Great Northern Railway, and, adjacent to the tracks, the Royal Canal, both spanned by a narrow bridge that led almost to the doorway of St. Laurence O'Toole's Catholic Church, the spire of which was plainly visible from the apartment. In back was a yard, containing a water-tap and toilet, which the Caseys shared — for the first time — with the Sheelds family downstairs. Beyond the yard stood the church. To the south, several blocks away, were the docks of the North Wall, where dimly-lighted river-front pubs beckoned to sailors, long-shoremen and cattle-drovers. Cattle-yards took up most of the space in between.

The neighborhood was quiet, intimate, and clean. It was shabbier than Hawthorne Terrace, but still it was not slum. Abercorn Road contained more houses like the Caseys', while on Church Street, around the corner, red-bricked cottages faced one another in two neat little rows. There were, in addition, some whitewalled cottages in the side avenue and alleyways nearby. Within, Susan Casey doughtily kept up appearances. The rooms were spotless, a cloth covered the kitchen table, and visitors were plied liberally with tea, bread, butter and jam. The chief difference between Hawthorne Terrace and Abercorn Road did not lie in tangibles. By sharing the house with another family, Susan Casey had suffered a subtle diminution in status, from rate-paying householder to ordinary tenant.

In October, 1899, Tom was recalled to active service as the Boer War began. It was only for a short time, as his term of enlistment would expire within the year, and — the autobiographies to the contrary — he was not shipped to the front. (Neither Tom nor Mick was ever stationed outside the United Kingdom.) Nevertheless his income must have been missed while he was away. Then, in April 1900, Susan Casey was dealt an even crueller blow when

Isaac married a frail Catholic girl named Johanna Fairtlough. The ceremony took place in Dublin's Procathedral, the entrance to which faced the Model Schools which had turned Isaac away without a diploma. Susan Casey did not attend. It did not help when her son converted to Catholicism himself, seizing upon the occasion to change his name from Isaac (which he had always despised) to Joseph

Materially Isaac had done well. His wife was from an old Norman family. Her parents maintained a chain of small grocery shops, which Isaac helped to manage. Her brother William later became prominent in labor and nationalist circles, holding numerous offices in Larkin's Transport and General Workers' Union. If Susan Casey thought her Isaac too good for Johanna, Johanna by all accounts thought herself too good for anyone, the Caseys included. O'Casey and Mick were commanded to wear collars and ties when they visited. O'Casey, the more bashful of the two, would redden and leave, but Mick would storm in unbidden, snarling that he was 'as good a man with a muffler.' And Isaac himself would greet Bella's children with a broad, conspiratorial wink and caution them — in tones imitative of Josie's carefully cultivated accent —'Now, boys and girls, we have to be precise.'

Through his indifferent efforts the business fared well enough for him to dress stylishly and drink often. He did both in respectable middle class fashion, wearing a grey suit and a soft grey hat which was pulled down over his eyes when he was drunk — the only visible sign that he'd had more than he could handle. He drank not only in the evenings but in the afternoons. Mostly he drank with Mick and Tom, who would meet him at the grocery shop, where he would withdraw enough money from the cash register to pay for the three of them. After several years of this the business began to go down-hill, and Isaac accepted a salaried position as clerk and salesman for the health insurance division of the Irish Transport and General Workers' Union. His wife's family probably had something to do with that also. Brother-in-law Willy was by then a member of the Union's central committee.

O'Casey didn't join his brothers when they went drinking together. It was probably fortunate that all were much older than he, so that they moved in different circles. Alone of the four boys, he'd acquired a lifelong aversion to hard liquor. Nor is it difficult to guess why. O'Casey had seen Isaac drink himself out of one good job after another, both before and during his marriage. Eventually he drank himself into a severe case of ulcers which shortened his life. Mick, whose relatives remember him as 'the real brains in the family,' was the heaviest drinker of the three. In his cups he would torment O'Casey with taunts and crude practical jokes. Tom, like Isaac, had a weak stomach and shouldn't have been drink-ing at all. But he wanted to keep up with Mick, and so he drank until he was ill. His nieces have always believed that his drinking contributed to his death, from peritonitis, at the early age of forty-five. Small wonder, therefore, that O'Casey himself was almost a teetotaler.

35

It is not clear precisely what O'Casey, now twenty years old, was doing when the century ended. It does not appear that he was working at any steady job. He had, however, become interested in the growing nationalist movement, which he served with his customary energy and enthusiasm.

Irish nationalism now claimed two distinct groups of adherents. One, ostensibly non-political, was dedicated to the revival of Irish language and culture. Its organized arm was the Gaelic League, founded in 1893 under the presidency of Douglas Hyde. The other was political, but within it there was a cleavage. In one camp was the Irish Parliamentary Party, committed to constitutional methods by its post-Parnellite leadership, and willing to settle for less than complete independence. In the other was the oathbound Irish Republican Brotherhood, whose members advocated total separation from Britain by physical force. Constitutionalism had always been alien to the Irish for want of an appropriate forum. Now, with the Parliamentary Party fractionalized and leaderless after Parnell's death, and frustrations mounting in the wake of repeated legislative rebuffs, the initative was rapidly passing to the militants.

O'Casey, like many of his contemporaries, moved in both circles. He had taught himself Irish and, at about the turn of the century, he joined the Lamh Dearh (Red Hand) branch of the Gaelic League, with headquarters in Drumcondra. He took up hurling, which he played with more gusto than skill, and regaled club members with humorous yarns about a mythical brother named Adolphus O'Casey, who seems to have been patterned after the real life Isaac. Adolphus was a social climber, a 'toff' who affected an upper class accent and pronounced his name O'Caysey. He opposed the activities of the Gaelic League, wooed the daughter of a prosperous grocer, and, after initial successes in love and finance, met disaster.

But the League was too tame to absorb all of O'Casey's energies. His Gaelic League activities caught the eye of some Fenians, and, at some undetermined date, O'Casey was inducted into the Teeling Circle of the Irish Republican Brotherhood. Mick, when he learned of it, snapped: 'You're finished. You've lost your freedom.'

In 1903, he went to work as a bricklayer's assistant for the Great Northern Railway. There he toiled nearly nine years, carrying tools and mixing concrete twelve hours a day, six days a week for a daily wage of three shillings. Scattered timesheets of his still turn up here and there, indicating the variety of tasks which he performed. For example, from September 19 until October 2, 1908, he worked at the power house in Sutton, adding parapet coping to the gables and repairing the roof. It was the only position which he was ever to hold for any substantial period.

Also in 1903, Tom, home from the army since November 1900, married a nearly illiterate Catholic servant-girl in a civil ceremony. Mary Kelly came from the Dublin suburb of Blackrock, where her father had been a plumber. To Susan Casey, this marriage was even more disagreeable than the others. She visited frequently with Isaac and Bella, and treated their spouses with courtesy if not with warmth. But she rarely set foot in Tom's home, and, while Tom came often to visit her, Mary always remained behind. No figure in the autobiographies — not schoolmaster Hogan, not even the minister whom O'Casey calls Hunter — is dealt with more harshly than Mary Casey. Moreover, O'Casey's relatives liked her no better than O'Casey did himself. The result is that it is impossible to arrive at a reliable judgment of the woman. One point, however, is clear: in terms of relative education, economic position, and social status, Tom married beneath him.

For, the marriage aside, Tom was doing quite well. He had been promoted by degrees to become head sorter on the Belfast mail train, and was about to step into an even higher position — head sorter on the mailboat which plied between Holyhead in Wales and Dublin's seaport of Dun Laoghaire — when his fatal illness struck him some years afterward. After his marriage, he moved first to Richmond Terrace, and then to Oxford Terrace, a pleasant avenue which runs into Hawthorne Terrace where the Caseys had once lived. Oxford, however, is by far the more fashionable of the two streets, with sturdy houses of brown brick, set off from the sidewalk by well-tended yards encased in wrought-iron fences.

Susan Casey avoided the place, but Mick didn't. Even O'Casey came along, and joined Mick and Tom in the singing of army songs, their favorite being *Let Me Like a Soldier Fall*. Sometimes he would follow shyly with a solo rendition of *The*

West's Awake or some other Irish patriotic air. And when Tom's two boys and a girl were older, he would give them arithmetic problems to solve, offering pennies for the right answer. One evening a large jug of stout fell to the floor and broke. Mick dropped on all fours to lap up the black liquid as it flowed from the jar.

Mary alone was excluded entirely from the family circle — or possibly she excluded herself. Otherwise the Caseys remained close even after the marriages. On Sundays they gathered for afternoon dinner, usually at the Beavers'. Tom and Mick would drift over several hours early, so that they could stroll through the country with Beaver while Beaver — a bird fancier who kept a large parrot at home — flew his pigeons. When O'Casey arrived later with his mother, he would settle himself in the best armchair, take a book from the shelf, and read placidly through the evening as the conversation swirled around him. Sometimes he would pause to sip at his cup of cocoa, which he prepared himself from a packet of chocolate which he carried in his pocket.

On afternoons the grandchildren — Bella's and, later, Tom's — visited Abercorn Road, where their grandmother greeted them in her spotless white apron. They had strict instructions to be quiet when their Uncle Jack was at home, and they tiptoed silently through the parlor in order not to disturb him while he was reading or writing. Often they found him practising on his bagpipes. O'Casey tried unsuccessfully to interest Tom's younger boy in those bagpipes when the youngster was nine years old. But

39

he gave it up as a hopeless task, for nine-year old Christopher Casey's attention was riveted instead on the silent cinema. 'You care more about Charlie Chaplin and Tom Mix,' his uncle scolded him, 'than SS. Peter and Paul.' O'Casey must have liked the sound of the phrase: some years afterward he inserted it, in only slightly altered form, into the mouth of Captain Boyle. But it wasn't only Christopher Casey who found the bagpipes distasteful. One night O'Casey blew on them till his lungs ached, and they gave forth no sound, for Mick had driven an awl through them earlier in the day.

Wherever the family assembled, Susan Casey presided. Serene and gentle in appearance, and outwardly cheerful, she was a hard woman when occasion required. Sundays she led her brood into church, where the family occupied almost an entire pew. She sat, lips compressed over toothless gums, her diminutive frame — less than five feet in height — invisible from the rear of the high-backed seats, alert for any fidgeting or untoward noise on the part of her grandchildren. Granny Casey had piercing eyes, which flashed fire when the youngsters misbehaved, and sometimes the flashes were followed by blows. Family dinners began with grace, and proceeded in virtual silence. Politics was one subject which was entirely prohibited. The brothers disagreed over politics, and Granny Casey would brook no dissension at her table. Mick in particular, deprecated O'Casey's nationalist activities, more out of combativeness than any deeply held conviction. 'Irish', he would growl when their mother wasn't present to interfere. 'What good's Irish in a British country?'

O'Casey continued to immerse himself in the projects of the Gaelic League, the Brotherhood, and the church. At St. Barnabas', Fletcher had been replaced by Rev. Edward Morgan Griffin. Already approaching forty when he was called to the parish, Griffin had entered the ministry only three years earlier, having taken his degree from Trinity in 1896. A disciplinarian in the classroom, he could bend sufficiently to pass out cakes to Catholic children who came to jeer at a church-sponsored lawn party. Whereas O'Casey and Fletcher had almost been contemporaries, O'Casey's relationship to Griffin was one of disciple to teacher. But for a time, at least, it was a close relationship nevertheless. After Sunday services, O'Casey regularly escorted Griffin's two oldest daughters home to the Rectory. Since Rutland Street lay directly along their route, Bella's children — of whom eventually there were five — often accompanied them. He dropped the youngsters off first, remained just long enough to mock playfully at the essays they were preparing for school, then continued west to 20 Charles Street, where the minister lived. He participated in prayer meetings, volunteering long, fervent prayers which others dreaded because of their length. At home visitors observed him poring over his bible.

He took to calling himself Sean O Cathasaigh, thus rendering his Christian and family names into Irish, and recruited energetically both for the Gaelic League and the Irish Republican Brotherhood. Liam

41

O Briain, who became a prominent educator, had taught himself Irish from a primer. O'Casey and a friend named Peter Nolan visited his home one evening to persuade him to join the League. O'Briain recalls that it was his first conversation in Irish, though he'd studied the language privately for years.

The Red Hand Branch to which O'Casey belonged fielded no hurling club, so he played for the Central Branch instead. A teammate was Ernest Blythe, who like himself had been relegated to the bench because of poor eyesight. Cautiously at first, O'Casey spoke to Blythe about the Fenians, then asked him bluntly if he wanted to join the I.R.B. 'I don't believe in assassination', said Blythe. 'We don't believe in assassination either,' O'Casey assured him. 'We're organizing for open warfare.' Convinced, Blythe submitted to induction.

The I.R.B. was not yet so active as it later became. Members' duties consisted chiefly of attending the monotonous monthly meetings, where they listened with little discussion to committee reports and messages from the mysterious Supreme Council, or talked of ways to raise money for the arms fund. At times their assignments were more diverting. An opposition group — the Parliamentary Party, for example — might try to hold a rally outside the Mansion House, where the mayor lived, and the Brotherhood would turn out to heckle the speakers and break up the gathering.

These exercises took up relatively little of O'Casey's time. Much of the remainder he devoted to both his deities at once, by campaigning to have

Anglican church services rendered into Irish. He was seconded by co-religionists Blythe and Seamas Deakin, another I.R.B. man, whose name appears frequently in the autobiographies. The three met in Deakin's flat above his large drugstore on O'Connell Street, where they were joined now and again by like-minded friends from the Brotherhood. There, during the winter of 1908, they drafted letters soliciting money for their various activities, which included inviting Irish-speaking ministers to preach at metropolitan churches and paying their travel expenses, or publishing portions of the Church of Ireland prayer book in Irish.

It was one task to obtain the necessary funds, and another to enlist the cooperation of hostile Protestant ministers. Sometimes O'Casey imperilled the project by giving voice to his high church learnings. The Rev. Phineas Hunt, for example, received him sympathetically until he spoke innocently of the 'priests' of the Church of Ireland. Hunt was low church, and the temperature in the room dropped noticeably. On another occasion, O'Casey stalked out of an Irish-language service after complaining that no psalms were being sung. Blythe, familiar with his friend's fierce temper, concluded that O'Casey had left in a fit of pique. When the psalm-singing began only a moment afterward, he scurried after him to bring him back. O'Casey, however, had left for a perfectly innocent reason: he had been taken suddenly ill.

O'Casey and Deakin saw a good deal of one another during the years 1908 through 1910. For about twelve months, beginning in 1909, the chemist shared his quarters with a nationalist intellectual named Bulmer Hobson. Often they invited the tall laborer for Saturday night supper, in part, Hobson recalls, because O'Casey was an entertaining talker, and in part because he looked as though he needed a meal. O'Casey's appearance must indeed have been frightening. Not only did he seem gaunt and ill-fed, but he had developed ingrown eyelashes which had to be plucked at regular intervals. In addition, his childhood disease still afflicted him, making his eyes red-rimmed and watery. All of this lent him a singularly fierce cast of expression. Nor was his expression altogether misleading. Hobson remembers that, for all his good humor, he often heaped violent abuse on people who disagreed with him. Hobson himself comes in for a share of that abuse in the autobiographies.

Not all O'Casey's fellow-Gaelic Leaguers were in sympathy with his Church-Irish activities. The socially pretentious, Protestant Five Provinces Branch frowned upon them as too radical and sectarian. Summoned to one of its meetings to defend himself, O'Casey deliberately appeared in a muffler instead of the usual collar and tie. However, this was an isolated episode, rather than a manifestation of the fierce proletarian outlook which he acquired afterward. He always wore a collar and tie to the meetings of his own Branch, though he dressed in shabby working-class garb at other times. Nor was there yet any trace of profound class consciousness in his self-deprecating humor. He mocked the wealthy casually, without apparent bitterness or deep conviction.

In 1909, the circle to which Blythe and O'Casey belonged was split into three sections, and the friends were separated. Blythe went to the north. Years later, after a colorful career as revolutionary and statesman, he became the director of the Abbey Theater which O'Casey had helped to rescue from bankruptcy.

From acquaintances here and there we get other glimpses of O'Casey in his mid-twenties — arguing the negative of the question, 'Resolved, that the Irish are unfit to rule themselves', before Protestant debating societies, where he was always able to draw a friendly laugh from a hostile audience; or browsing through Webb's Bookstore, on the south quay, where Stephen Synott worked as a clerk. It was in 1905, when Synott was first hired, that he began to notice the tall, shabbily-dressed figure, clad in hobnailed boots and a muffler and wearing spectacles, who appeared about twice a week to purchase cheap or second-hand books. After a while Synott came to know his tastes, and would set aside his favorites: Dostoievsky, Chekhov, Ibsen, or a Chambers dictionary or occasional English grammar. Often they talked together, mostly about books, never about politics. O'Casey expressed vehement dislike for Brinsley MacNamara, a free-thinking author who had became a Catholic, and for all persons who wrote without knowing their subjects. Many years later, when O'Casey was a world-renowned playwright, Synott encountered him on one of his infrequent visits to Dublin. 'You don't like people who write things they don't know about', Synott reminded him. 'What do you know about Railway Street?' Railway Street, one-time center of Dublin's red light district, was the site of the now-demolished Shanahan's Pub, which is featured in *The Plough and the Stars*. O'Casey replied that he'd spent a month in Shanahan's, gathering dialogue and atmosphere for the play.

In 1905, or thereabouts — nobody knows exactly when — Susan Casey celebrated her seventieth birthday 'Mother', said Mick dolefully, 'we'll have to shoot you.' The family was reasonably comfortable, more so, probably, than at any time since the father's death. O'Casey was working. Mick was almost certainly still employed by the Post Office, and judging from its salary schedules was earning enough to support his mother, his brother and himself. To be sure, he was drinking heavily, but neighbors and relatives attest that he also contributed generously to the upkeep of the others. Tom and Isaac were also living comfortably in their separate households, as were the Beavers.

According to his daughters, Nicholas Beaver had not done badly. From porter on the Great Northern Railway he had become, first a ticket collector and then the head of the parcel office. Like his in-laws, he strove fiercely to keep up appearances. His income couldn't have amounted to much for a married man with five children, but he set aside enough of it to put his oldest child Susan through the Central Model

Schools. She was nearing sixteen, an age at which working-class progeny were already employed. But her parents had ordained that she be reared as a lady, and not be permitted to work.

Then, in 1905, Beaver was hospitalized with a slow, crippling illness which physicians diagnosed as paralysis of the brain. Bella moved with her brood into a shabby tenement house on Fitzgibbon Street, where she managed for a time on her husband's scanty savings. She was there on November 10, 1907, when Beaver, not quite forty years old, succumbed in Richmond Hospital. Soon afterward, her savings ran out, she had to leave Fitzgibbon Street, and she came with her five children to live with her grandmother on Abercorn Road.

It was only a temporary arrangement, to last until she found new quarters of her own. While it continued, however, the Caseys and Beavers were living like working-class families in Dublin's Georgian tenements, with nine people packed somehow into two small bedrooms, the children sleeping on the floors. After two or three months of this, Bella found a small cottage around the corner in Brady's Lane, where George Middleton had battled as a schoolboy to protect O'Casey from neighborhood bullies. Once again, however, she was unable to keep up the rent. This time she was evicted, and had to endure the humiliation of having her belongings put out into street. (Actually, it may have been the second time. O'Casey describes a similar occurrence in *Drums Under the Windows*, which — to judge from the landmarks he identifies — would have taken place at

Fitzgibbon Street.) A neighbor who owned some small houses in nearby Church Place gave her the use of a vacant one-room cottage. There she lived for six months, rent-free, until she was able at last to afford a somewhat larger house next door. To find the wherewithal to pay the weekly rent of four shillings, she took to scrubbing floors three or four times a week, earning a shilling each time. Mostly she worked for her neighbor Mrs. Irvine, who owned a row of cottages in Brady's Lane. She never tried to go back to teaching. Her spirit was broken, say her daughters, and she lacked the will to make the necessary effort. This conforms to the portrait which O'Casey paints of his sister, listless and prematurely aged.

On January 1, 1909, the British government instituted an old age pension plan. Susan Casey, already well past the minimum age of seventy, qualified for the maximum allotment: five shillings a week. This was because she had no other income except for contributions from her children, which were not counted. When the first check arrived, Mick chortled approvingly. 'That's a feather in your cap, Mother,' he said.

O'Casey in 1909 was drifting between old and new enthusiasms. He had severed his ties with St. Barnabas' a year or two earlier, having taken exception, some say, when the vestry ordered an English-made organ. Others, less plausibly, have him stalking off in a huff after Griffin hoisted a Union Jack to celebrate the king's birthday, vowing 'I wouldn't go to a church that flies a bloody rag like that.' But he wasn't long in finding other interests. In 1908, James Larkin had come from Liverpool to organize the Irish Workers' Union, soon to become O'Casey's new church militant. At about the same time — 1907 or 1908 — he attended a Gaelic League meeting at which he met Frank Cahill, teacher at the Christian Brothers' School of St. Laurence O'Toole's, and co-founder of the Laurence O'Toole Club.

The Club, established in 1901, was among the first of several to organize during the early years of the twentieth century. There was nothing clandestine about them. In structure they were ordinary social groups, but their social activities were changed with nationalist overtones: Irish dancing, for example. From their precincts came the young men who later fought during Easter Week, the War of Independence, and the Civil War. Cahill, himself an ardent nationalist, had marked the more promising among his schoolboys and guided them, first into the Club and later into the Irish Republican Brotherhood.

O'Casey and Cahill quickly became friends. In addition to being a nationalist, the schoolmaster possessed an insatiable curiosity about his fellow mortals and a rare gift for mimicry. His curiosity took him frequently to Dublin's criminal courts, where he watched from the spectator's section as the Rosie Redmonds and the Coveys passed before the bar. Then, on weekends, he and O'Casey would stroll together along the Royal Canal, bringing their lunches with them, while Cahill spun stories of what

49

he had seen. These walks lasted the better part of the day. Often, after they had returned, the two would stand outside Cahill's house and talk until two or three in the morning. If Cahill was a remarkable yarn-spinner, O'Casey was a patient listener, and — as we have seen — was blessed with an unusually retentive memory besides. He took no notes of their many conversations, but he paid close attention to what was said, interrupting occasionally to ejaculate, 'Ah, there's a good one, Frank!' Years later, according to O'Tooles who knew them both, some of Cahill's anecdotes found their way onto the Abbey stage.

With Cahill, O'Casey helped to organize the St. Laurence O'Toole's Pipers Band, which is today the oldest such band in the city. In 1910, when it first made its appearance, its members marched in kilts knitted by Cahill's sister, and practised under the tutelage of a flute-player, no piper being available to instruct them. O'Casey played the pipes about as well as he wielded a hurling stick. As a result, he seldom participated in the band's performances, and never when it was engaged in competitions. But as its secretary, he scheduled its appearances, took charge of publicity, and accompanied it wherever it went. In fact, the secretary was for practical purposes the leader of the enterprise. The presidency, a strictly honorary position involving only nominal duties, was to be conferred upon a leading nationalist, whose name could raise the band to prominence, secure for it invitations to perform at important functions, and facilitate its fund-raising.

O'Casey knew such a man. He was Tom Clarke, one of the Irish Republican Brotherhood's few surviving links with the rebels of an earlier generation. He had recently returned from America, where he'd settled briefly after spending half a lifetime in British prisons. His confinement had left him out of touch with the national movement, and now to his chagrin he found himself scorned as a latecomer to its ranks by some of his own contemporaries. They in turn seemed too cautious and timid to Clarke. In 1908 he had opened a pair of shops in Amiens Street, not far from the Club's first headquarters in Oriel Place, and in 1910 he moved his business across town to 75a Parnell Square. At each location there gathered many of the Brotherhood's younger spirits, chafing like Clarke himself under the restraints imposed by the older members.

O'Casey's acquaintance with Clarke dated at least from 1910, when Clarke's wife first noticed him coming to Parnell Street to talk politics with the old Fenian. He spoke little to her, giving her only a curt nod as she stood behind the counter, and leaving with a shrug of his shoulders when Clarke was not in. But her husband took a liking to the tall laborer, who discharged without pay or publicity such menial tasks as the loading and unloading of the magaizne *Irish Freedom*, which Clarke sold at his shop. Later, after O'Casey had left the Brotherhood, Clarke would describe him in a letter as 'a disgruntled fellow.' For the present, however, he praised him to his wife as a man who 'put Ireland first'. He accepted the presidency of the Pipers, and the band prospered.

Larkin's union, founded in 1909, had meanwhile changed its name to the Irish Transport and General Workers' Union as it opened its ranks to all the laboring classes. From a small furnished office it moved into a reconverted hotel beside the Liffey, which its leaders rechristened Liberty Hall. It is not clear at what time O'Casey actually joined the union. But by 1911 he adhered to it at least in spirit, and this did not sit well with his employers on the Great Northern Railway.

His association with the railroad had been unsatisfactory from his standpoint and from theirs. He gave the impression of resenting his superiors, from the white collar clerical personnel to his immediate supervisor, Foreman Reid. One alone he acknowledged: P. A. Foley, a traffic supervisor, to whom he barked a reluctant greeting in Irish, but only because he knew that Foley had been taking Irish lessons himself.

He received orders with little grace, and reprimands — which were frequent — with less. Foley, one of his superiors, reports that he got on poorly with his fellow workers, which sounds credible enough, since he and they had little in common. It was not that O'Casey was truculent or aggressive. He simply didn't care to be bothered. Often he would stand in the midst of a group, leaning on his shovel and staring off into space, affecting complete indifference to the conversation around him.

Some of his resentment was directed against the small-time graft which was practised by the foremen. Reid, for example, demanded a commission before he permitted his workers to borrow company tools for private use. Others paid off without protest. O'Casey, typically, would not.

His nationalism involved him in a running feud with the management, loyalist to a man. He studied Irish ostentatiously during his work breaks. He changed his name from John Casey to John O'Casey and finally to Sean O Cathasaigh. When the company proclaimed a holiday on the coronation day of George V, O'Casey reported for work. When it paid its workmen for the holiday, he refused to accept the money.

In 1911, the company established a pension fund, financed in part out of compulsory contributions by its employees. The plan received the hearty approbation of the National Union of Railwaymen, a yea-saying body to which all railway workers, O'Casey included, belonged. But Larkin's union opposed the scheme, and O'Casey refused to participate.

He and the Great Northern Railway had at last run out of patience with one another. On November 28, he was given two weeks' notice. A lengthly correspondence followed, in which O'Casey demanded, not reinstatement, but an opportunity to refute at a hearing charges of 'habitual neglect of work' which had been levelled against him by Foreman Reid. These charges, which constituted the ostensible reason for his dismissal, O'Casey dismissed as a subterfuge 'generated by a strong desire on the part of Foreman

Reid to separate me from the company.' Secretary of the Railway Morrison passed O'Casey's letter on to Chief Engineer Campion, who invited Engineer Whieldon — from whom the dimissal order had issued — to submit a memorandum. In the memorandum, Whieldon acknowledged that O'Casey had been discharged for refusing to join the pension fund. '(I)n addition,' Whieldon reported, 'his eyesight is defective and it is doubtful if the Company's Doctor would pass him — further he is inclined to be idle and has been warned on several occasions.' O'Casey was dissatisfied with the company's reply, and again pressed Morrison to grant him a hearing. On December 21, Campion advised Morrison that 'there is no other reply to be given to O'Casey further than to the effect that the Company have no longer use for his services.' That closed the matter.

There is one further point to be made, and that is that the above mentioned exchange of letters contradicts O'Casey's own account of his dismissal. In *Drums Under the Windows*, he writes that he was fired when he refused to sign a document circulated by the Dublin Employer's Federation, requiring all employees to forswear allegiance to Larkin's Union. Such a document was indeed distributed, but not until two years afterward, in the wake of the transport strike of 1913. Clearly, therefore, it cannot have been a factor in his discharge.

The reader should also remember that this was the period when O'Casey was laboring without pay as one of the 'faceless volunteers' who delivered the magazine *Irish Freedom* to Tom Clarke's bookshop.

Years afterward, Mrs. Clarke read the autobiographies and marvelled that O'Casey, out of work, had never discussed his plight with Clarke or other nationalist leaders, any one of whom would readily have procured him some compensation for his services. She didn't know O'Casey, who would sooner have starved than begged for assistance.

In 1913 came the first test of strength between Larkin and the Employers' Federation. It began on August 26, the first day of the Horse Show, premier event of Dublin's social season. At 10 a.m., the tram workers abruptly abandoned their trolleys, leaving the gentry and their ladies to continue to the show on foot. Clerical employees left their desks to man the trams under police protection. Larkin proclaimed a mass rally in O'Connell Street, to take place the following Sunday, the 31st. When the authorities banned it, Larkin vowed to speak anyway.

A huge crowd poured into O'Connell Street that Sunday morning to see whether he would keep his promise. Many were striking workers, but some — such as Mick — were merely curious. At 1.30, Larkin stepped out onto the balcony of the Imperial Hotel, disguised as a bearded clergyman. Just as he began to speak, police dragged him back into the room and placed him under arrest, while, on the streets, their comrades charged into the crowd with raised truncheons. 'Bloody Sunday' marked the beginning of a strike which dragged on through the winter and into the early months of 1914. In the end, it was inconclusive. The employers did not succeed in crushing the union, but neither were they compelled to recognize it. Perhaps its most important consequence was that the brutality of law-enforcement officials, from the magistrates down to the police, had convinced many — O'Casey among them — that the workers had no other recourse than a fighting force of their own.

O'Casey had looked to the Irish Republican Brotherhood to supply such a force. But its leaders were reluctant to involve the national movement in the class struggle. Some feared that involvement would breed divisiveness; others, employers themselves, were openly hostile to labor. The result was that O'Casey walked out of the Brotherhood late in 1913, taking several others with him. (This fact led some of his friends to believe that he had held office in the organization. They were mistaken. O'Casey indeed commanded a following, but this was owing exclusively to the force of his personality.)

Denied the support of the nationalists, the workers' army mobilized on its own. In October, 1913, at the very height of the strike, Larkin, James Connolly, and a soldier of fortune named Jack White founded the Irish Citizen Army. Its troops drilled openly in Croydon Park, using broomsticks instead of guns, or sometimes hurling clubs, which — unlike broomsticks — could kill. The Citizen Army did not remain for long the only private military corps in the south of Ireland. Already it had been anticipated in the north by Ulster loyalists, who had organized the Ulster Volunteers to resist home rule if it ever came.

This was a signal to nationalists in the south, who reasoned that if Ulster could arm, so could they. In November 1913, a month after the founding of the Citizen Army, the Irish Republican Brotherhood joined forces with nationalists of all complexions to establish the Irish Volunteers. The two little armies mistrusted each other. When the Volunteers smuggled rifles into Dublin through Howth Harbor in July, 1914, they refused to share them with the Citizen Army. But a number of weapons were lost in transit, and Citizen Army men picked up the leavings. Now both units possessed arms, and drilled openly, fearing neither the police nor one another. Meanwhile, a small but militant group of I.R.B. men was plotting to seize control of the Volunteers under the very noses of their more consrvative commanders.

The Citizen Army captured O'Casey's imagination. In March, 1914, he took an active role in its re-organization: a re-organization which included the implementation of systematic drills, division into companies, the creation of an executive council and, finally, a constitution which he drafted himself. On March 22 he was elected secretary of the Army, a position which gave him a seat on the executive council. One of his first acts was to challenge Volunteer President Eoin MacNeill to debate with him 'the ambiguous provisions of the Volunteer constitution and the class basis of the Provisional Executive.' MacNeill replied that he knew of no such class distinctions in his organization, and could not discuss a subject of which he was ignorant.

The most important of his duties, however, was

recruitment. In the Spring of 1914 he sat at a table with Seamas McGowan, who later chased butterflies at Knocksedan in *Shadow of a Gunman*. Frank Robbins, not yet out of his teens, approached them. Addressing himself to O'Casey, he inquired timidly, 'Please, sir, may I join the Irish Citizen Army?' The youngster was afraid he didn't qualify. He was slight of stature, and Larkin, in one of his typically flamboyant speeches, had called for men who were 'six feet tall.' O'Casey quickly reassured him. 'Certainly,' he said heartily, 'you're just the sort of man we're looking for.' Standing in the shadow of Butts Bridge, adjacent to Liberty Hall, he spoke fiercely to listening workers, admonishing them that 'votes never won a war.' Often he ranged beyond Dublin in his search for soldiers, going once to Dun Laoghaire, some ten miles away. When he returned he reported to the membership that the only way to stimulate interest was through uniforms. If Robbins heard it correctly, the report was inconsistent with O'Casey's autobiographical assertion that he advocated guerrilla warfare and scorned uniforms, open drill, and massed battle formations.

Paddy Buttner was too young to join the Citizen Army until after O'Casey had left it. But the tall, muffler-clad ex-laborer with the shuffling gait and red-rimmed watery eyes came frequently to his father's barber shop across the river, where he discussed politics with other customers, many of them Citizen Army men themselves. It was O'Casey who did most of the talking, while the rest listened respectfully. It was clear to Buttner that they liked him, and even looked to him for leadership.

O'Casey's association with the Citizen Army was short lived. Two factions were emerging within the organization, one of which favored closer co-operation with the Volunteers. Among its more vocal spokesmen was Countess Constance Markievicz, who was also associated with the Volunteers through her membership in its women's auxilary, Cumann na mBan. O'Casey himself had taken the same position before the Irish Republican Brotherhood, and had broken with the Brotherhood when it rebuffed him. Now, with the memory of that rebuff still fresh, he opposed any form of co-operation, maintaining that the British and Volunteers alike were enemies and oppressors.

In August, 1914, he rose at an Army meeting in Liberty Hall and proposed a resolution, calling upon the Countess to sever her ties with one group or the other. The immediate issue was only symbolic. The real issue was the direction which the Citizen Army would take in years to come. According to Robbins, O'Casey defended his proposal with such fervor that he quarrelled on the floor with Larkin, and left the meeting with several of his friends before the Evecutive Committee voted. What is certain is that the Committee decided, by the margin of a single ballot, to support the Countess; it was her own vote that broke the tie. O'Casey on the other hand abstained, if indeed he was present at all.

The upshot of the episode was that O'Casey severed his connection with the Army, and began gradually to drop away from the union itself. Quite apart from his quarrel with the Countess, he no longer enjoyed the confidence of the inner leadership. Larkin, his friend, left for America in October of 1914. The men who took Larkin's place were more clerical, less radical, and more conciliatory to the Volunteers. But he still came to Liberty Hall He and his followers, outsiders now like himself, congregated on the steps to discuss their views; others derisively nicknamed them 'the Steps Committee.' And he must have retained at least some of his friends on the inside as well. In the summer of 1915, he required an operation for tuberculosis of the neck. Beds were scarce because of the war, and it was the union which arranged his admission to St. Vincent's Hospital, where according to hospital records he remained from August 15 until September 1.

On February 6, 1914, Thomas Casey died Of O'Casey's three brothers, he had always been the steadiest: a willing worker and devoted husband and father. Separated from the army for the last fourteen years of his life, he'd never lost his martial appearance. The drooping mustache, the crisp manner of speaking, even his choice of words (he always preferred the military term 'biscuits' to 'sweets') all suggested the soldier. He was a kindly man, too. Once, deputized to send the traditional wreath to the wife of a departed post office colleage, he'd travelled all the way across town to deliver it in person.

Tom, like his father before him, had lived to the limits of his means. His estate contained a scanty five pounds. There were death benefits from the Post Office, but these disappeared quickly, and Mary — like Bella — took to scrubbing floors. Her two boys went through military school on scholarships granted to soldiers' orphans. The elder made a career of the army — he was a drummer, as his uncle Nicholas Beaver had been — while the younger became a dockhand.

O'Casey's own account of Tom's death is flatly contradicted by both boys, who have no reason to conceal the truth. He was not present at the death-bed, as he claimed to have been, nor do the children, who were, recall any visit by Rev. Griffin. Nevertheless, he renders eloquent tribute to Tom in the autobiographies, and in *Juno and the Paycock* he proffers a more subtle salute to the memory of his favorite brother. The famous will in that play is dated February 6.

Now that O'Casey had parted, successively, with the Church, his job, the I.R.B. and the Citizen Army, his life revolved almost entirely around the Club. As secretary of its Pipers Band — a position which he probably retained until late 1914 — he displayed the same talents for oratory and administration which had raised him to prominence in labor circles. To publicize the band's activities, he organized public rallies, securing as speakers such leading nationalists as Douglas Hyde and Patrick Pearse. At one rally, a friend recalls, he introduced Hyde and Pearse to the audience, and, after their speeches, accepted a flag from them on behalf of the band. He himself was a prolific and persuasive speaker at the club's semi-annual business meetings. He even had occasion once to try his talents in court. Returning one Sunday morning from Bodenstown, where they had marched to render homage at the grave of Irish martyr Wolfe Tone, band members taunted their police escort by playing *The Peeler and the Goat* — a derisive ballad of a police officer who arrested a goat for high treason. The sergeant in command bided his time until the band swung past a church, then slapped it with a summons for interrupting Sunday services. The summons was issued to O'Casey, who answered the sergeant in Irish. But when he appeared in court to speak for himself and his comrades, he was much subdued. He patiently told the judge, who had heard only of fife and drum bands, just what a pipe band was; then assured his lordship that no disrespect could possibly have been intended, since the church was none other than St. Mary's, where O'Casey had been baptized. The summons was dismissed.

He delighted in playing devil's advocate during informal discussions at the club. Irish, he taunted a new member, was 'a damn language, dead as so-and-so'; why should anyone want to bother learning it? He discussed books with enthusiasm, usually taking the opposite point of view from whomever happened to be speaking. On the rare occasions when someone mentioned a book he hadn't read himself, he was certain to read it within a few days, in order to debate its merits when it next came up for discussion. Not all his contentiousness was friendly banter. Some of the O'Tooles were natty dressers; O'Casey ridiculed them as 'gentleman-printers' (one was indeed a printer.) They nearly had their revenge when O'Casey was playfully locked out of the club one evening and failed to appreciate the joke. Scrambling in at last through an open window, he swore at the instigators so roundly that he was hauled before the executive committee, where the 'gentleman-printers' sought his expulsion. But O'Casey soothed most of the membership with a gracious apology, much as he had placated the judge in magistrate's court. The anecdote illustrates three of his more prominent characteristics: his temper, his gift of diplomacy (when he chose to exercise it), and his propensity for coarseness. The latter was sometimes apparent in his humor also, as when he stood with the band in a driving rain and a flippant soul leaned out a window to inquire about the weather. It was wet, snapped O'Casey in Irish. The Irish word for wet is pronounced 'fluc.'

He followed a fairly regular routine. In the early afternoon he would shuffle across the bridge which leads from Abercorn Road to St. Laurence O'Toole's, on his way to the Christian Brothers' school where Frank Cahill taught. They met after classes and walked together to Cahill's house on the North Strand, where they took their midday meal. They sat at the table, the schoolmaster and the tall ex-laborer, discussing the affairs of the club. Then, when dinner was over, they would go to Oriel Street or Seville Place or wherever the club had its

63

headquarters at the time. Almost every evening, O'Casey would wander down to the Five Lamps, at the head of Seville Street: a streetcorner named for the five street lamps which hung there. Here he would meet his close friend Paddy McDonnell, fifteen years younger than himself. From the Five Lamps they would go off on long walks down Malahide Road, sometimes just the two of them, sometimes in the company of two or three friends from the club. During these walks O'Casey expounded on his favorite authors: Burns, Shaw, Jack London. Shaw in particular he admired. McDonnell remembers that he quoted from his works constantly.

Wednesday and Sunday nights were *ceilidh* nights, when the O'Tooles and their girls danced to Irish music. O'Casey often entertained them by singing a traditional ballad or song he'd written himself. But he cut an awkward figure on the dance floor, where he tramped about self-consciously in his hobnailed boots. The girls, most of them much younger than he was, thought him puzzling, and not all of them liked him. To Cahill's niece Josie Daly he paid flowery compliments, unusual in a man of that period. 'Ah, you have lovely hair, Josie,' he would tell her. Stephen Synnott's fiancee danced with him only to be polite, finding him a clumsy partner and a reticent conversationalist. The result was that he dated seldom. The night that Douglas Hyde returned from a triumphant tour of America, the O'Tooles piped him to the Mansion House. There was a *ceilidh* afterward, and when it was over the pipers dispersed, each with a girl on his arm, while O'Casey

64

staggered home alone, bearing on his shoulders the band's huge drum.

His appearance was sufficiently unusual so that both friends and casual acquaintances recall it vividly. Standing to his full height, he was well over six feet, and even when he slouched, as he generally did, he towered over his companions. At thirty-five he was still lean of figure, more so than ever in recent years, for he hadn't been eating well since he'd stopped working. Besides, he'd been ill, and in and out of hospitals with one ailment or another. Friends pitied the gaunt ex-laborer, so obviously sick and apparently hungry too. One made the error of arranging a job for him in the stockroom of the Irish Independent. 'I don't need any job,' O'Casey snapped when the news was brought to him. But to Paddy McDonnell he confided that he hadn't eaten meat in five years. Most remarkable were his eyes. They were angry-looking, but not from fierceness of disposition, nor even from too much writing and study under a dim light. They were red-rimmed and watery from the childhood disease which still tormented him.

He was shabbily dressed, unlike his brother Mick, who was always careful of his appearance. Some thought it an affectation, the way he'd tramp about in those hobnailed boots of his, even on the dance floor at St. Laurence O'Tooles, when a *ceilidh* was in progress. Outdoors he wore a heavy muffler, probably to protect his neck, where he'd had his operation, and sometimes a baggy raincoat. He had, as well, an ungraceful, shuffling manner of walking, and in all

65

resembled a peculiarly ill-favored scarecrow. Street urchins would accost the apparition and ask him the time, not because they really wanted to know, but because they were fascinated by his strange attire, and wanted to hear him answer them — as he always did — in Irish.

There is, on the other hand, sharp disagreement about his personality. Strangers were put off by his manner and appearance. He was gruff, sometimes moody, and a few even called him sullen. Stephen Synnott, the bookstore clerk who later joined the O'Tooles, thought him solemn and humorless. To Josie Daly he remained a puzzling figure, at times a lively conversationalist, yet at other times given to sitting and staring at some distant object, especially after someone had contradicted him. Others had marked this habit of his, railway supervisor Foley among them. His neighbors on Abercorn Road took little notice of him, one way or the other. There was something about him which did not encourage them to venture a closer acquaintance. They felt far more comfortable with Mick, who would joke with them and drink with them, and they left his younger brother alone. Yet for all O'Casey's aloofness — a composite of pride and reticence — he possessed an easy, almost regal courtesy. It wasn't enough to endear him to the neighbors, but it won him at least their respect and approbation.

One derives a very different picture from his small circle of intimate friends. Most of these were many years his junior, but were nevertheless among the older members of the club. They found him neither

66

sullen nor moody. Instead, they marvelled at his hearty sense of humor, free from any taint of hostility or self-pity, in the face of poverty and illness. He had, John MacDonald remembers, a booming laugh which, together with his singing, made him 'the life and soul' of *ceilidhs* and informal gatherings at the club. Since he was so much older than they, they came to him with their problems. He listened patiently, and sometimes did more than listen, as when he 'beat his brains out'— Paddy McDonnell's expression — to obtain a pension for Frank Cahill's sister, widowed while her husband was in the Navy.

O'Casey wasn't schizoid. The various descriptions of him are entirely compatible, representing as they do the conflicting impressions of strangers who judged on the basis of external appearances, and close friends who knew their subject well.

When Larkin left for America, James Connolly succeeded him as Irish Citizen Army commander. By 1915, he had cast his lot decisively with the Volunteers, and had even joined the Irish Republican Brotherhood. The two units now drilled openly together, defying the authorities, who chose in turn to ignore them. In complacency the British were outdone only by the Volunteer executive, whose following was being wrested away from it by a determined band of fanatics, bent on martyrdom.

Too late, Volunteer President MacNeill awoke to what was happening. The Rising had been scheduled to begin on Easter Sunday, 1916. MacNeill, alerted only the day before, issued countermanding orders. But he succeeded only in postponing the rebellion for one day, and, in the ensuing confusion, depriving the rebels of support from the countryside. On Easter Monday, combined Volunteer and Citizen Army units occupied the General Post Office and other strategic points around the city.

O'Casey, of course, wasn't among them, having retired from the struggle nearly two years earlier. Neither was O'Casey's old comrade Seamas Deakin, who had risen to the Supreme Council of the Irish Republican Brotherhood, then had left the movement abruptly in 1914. Nor was their erstwhile dinner companion Bulmer Hobson, now secretary of the Volunteers and MacNeill's second-in-command, whom rebel leaders had kidnapped to prevent him from frustrating their plans.

But there were other friends of his who did fight: Jimmy Shiels, and Johnny MacDonald, both from the club. Johnny's brother Paddy had stayed at home, but not because he wanted to. The boys had agreed that one of them should remain to support the family if the other were killed. Then there was Mick Smith, stationed inside Jacob's Biscuit Factory, which the rebels had occupied at the onset of the fighting. From time to time he peered cautiously outside, where he could see clearly through the window of the flat across the street. All week long a tiny coffin had lain there — a child's coffin, to judge from the size of it. The family didn't dare venture out of doors to bury it. Smith found the sight profoundly moving. After the Rising had ended in failure, and he had returned from a British prison camp, he joined the O'Tooles' Club, where he recounted many times the story of the coffin. Years later, he watched a performance of *the Plough and the Stars*. When the curtain rose on the final act, he saw Mollser's coffin on the stage, and he thought suddenly of another coffin he had seen.

Though O'Casey was not a participant, neither he nor anyone else in Dublin could avoid involvement. On Thursday night, when the Rising was four days old, British troops ranged through the neighborhood to round-up suspected nationalist sympathizers. O'Casey's name was known to the authorities as a result of his earlier activities, and he was herded with the others into St. Barnabas' church, where they were locked up for the night. On Friday morning, they were permitted to go home, but on Friday night a Welsh regiment with Welsh-speaking soldiers went from door to door, arresting every adult male in the area. The internees were deposited in the cellar of a huge granary nearby, where they remained until Saturday morning, playing cards and chatting with the soldiers and seeing, in the distance, a faint glow as O'Connell Street went up in flames. 'Will we have to come back tonight?' asked one of O'Casey's companions as the soldiers released them. A Tommy sang out, 'If we want you, we'll fetch you.' But by Saturday night no fetching was needed. The rebels had surrendered.

MacDonald and Shiels marched with their fellow-prisoners through sullen streets packed with jeering, often angry crowds, to ships which would carry them to British detention camps. O'Casey did not forget them. He wrote to them often, enclosing with his letters cleverly drawn cartoons, in which he conveyed current news, or else depicted his lonliness during their absence. To MacDonald he sent a caricature of himself, standing alone and dejected on Annesley Bridge with a cigarette trailing from his mouth. Shiels received a drawing of civilians dodging bullets during the Rising; another portraying the looting of shops, in which a policeman looks on in amazement as a shabbily dressed Dubliner enters a store and emerges a moment later clad in an expensive suit; and still a third showing Frank Cahill collecting money for a prisoners' aid fund while slyly eyeing a pretty female co-worker. It was, O'Casey wrote Shiels, 'a sketch of "Dear Francis", collecting on the Quays for the National Aid Association ("Cumann Casanta na nGaedhael") with a sweet little colleen.' Shiels evidently found the cartoon amusing, for in a later letter O'Casey wrote: 'Sorry to read that my "sketch" of "Frank and Somebody Else" was a source of enjoyment. Viewed in the "Perspective"— to use a war expert term — it is a cause for heart searching and general deprecation. However, I have spoken to Father Breen about the matter, and he promised to speak to Frank seriously about his un-edifying and reprehensible conduct.' Dublin, he declared, was much the same:

Clergy preach; the Salvation Army still trolls out under the Customs House Bridge: 'Glory for me, glory for me, that'll be glory, glory for me!' The pubs are doing their best to satisfy their patrons; the children in the slums still run around naked and hungry; the hospitals and the theatres are always full; and the sneering moon looks down and laughs quietly at us all. Oh! Life, Life! Oh, man, oh, man! Today a worm; tomorrow a god; today a god; tomorrow a worm again.

Just as you say, Seamas, I try to laugh at the world — nay, I do not laugh *at* the world, but with the world, for a cheerful spirit will serve a man in Heaven or in Hell.

That summer, Cahill took advantage of the long vacation to smuggle about ten of the rebels who had escaped imprisonment out of the city to Curraghtown, in County Meath. There they pitched tents on a large meadow owned by Cahill's cousin, and lay low while police raided their Dublin homes. O'Casey accompanied them. He had no job to keep him in Dublin, and the idea of camping appealed to him. Cahill, conditioned to urban amenities, slept comfortably in his cousin's house, but O'Casey stayed with the men. Once, hearing Cahill spin stories of hoboes, he murmured, 'That's the life for you and me, Frank', and he drew another cartoon for Johnny MacDonald, depicting himself and Cahill as hoboes around a campfire.

In July, 1915, Mick enlisted in his old outfit, the Inland Water Corps of the Royal Engineers. A source of irritation was gone; so, however, was a source of support. Since relevant Post Office records have been destroyed, one cannot say whether Mick had been working there or elsewhere. Whatever he'd been doing, he'd supplied all of the family income, except only for his mother's old age pension. Moreover, visitors to the house insist that, of the two brothers, Mick was the more attentive to their mother, Mick the one who ran errands and helped to clean the home.

Just as no-one knows where Mick had been working, no-one knows either how much he'd been earning, or how much of his salary he'd been contributing to the upkeep of the others. O'Tooles who were closest to O'Casey surmise from his appearance that the family was hard-pressed even before Mick's departure. However, he never discussed his finances with any of them, apart from the one instance when he'd confided to Paddy McDonnell that he hadn't eaten meat in five years. Neighbors and relatives, on the other hand, maintain that the Caseys had lived comfortably, if modestly. O'Casey himself records that they had purchased their food at Murphy's shop on Church Street, and fifty years later Murphy's daughter still remembers that they had paid their weekly bills regularly. Whatever their circumstances before 1915, it seems certain that O'Casey and his mother had no source of income thereafter other than her old age pension and whatever moneys Mick was sending home from his army paycheck. Since he was earning, at the very most, a shilling and ten pence a day as a private in the Royal Engineers, it is reasonable to conclude that their weekly income cannot possibly have exceeded fifteen shillings. This was meager fare even for working class families of the period.

Then, later that year — or possibly early in the following one — Isaac fled from Dublin.

The Irish Transport and General Workers Union had treated him well. As a sales clerk in its Health Insurance section, he'd earned enough to put his children through the Model Schools, and clothe himself in the conservative yet stylish suits he'd always fancied. His first love was still the stage, and in his spare time he had helped to organize the Liberty Hall Players, the union's dramatic society. He posessed what a niece later called a theatrical personality, by which she meant that he sang and play-acted off the stage as well as on it. He also had a high opinion of his own talents, which his fellow-actors did not share. He refused to learn his lines, insisting instead upon dubbing in his own, and he made his entrances whenever he chose, often from the wrong side of the stage. These practises embroiled him in frequent quarrels with the director, and culminated in his leaving the Players early in 1916.

Like Tom, he had abused an already weak stomach by drinking heavily in his younger years. By 1916 he had developed ulcers so severe that he virtually subsisted on bicarbonate of soda. His most serious problem of all, however, was not a weak stomach but a soft heart.

Isaac was the sort of man who couldn't say no to people. He couldn't say no to Mick and Tom when they'd coaxed him away from his shop to go drinking with them. He couldn't say no when they'd suggested

73

that he raid the till to pay their way through the pubs. Now, as an insurance clerk, he couldn't say no to clients who wanted him to release maternity benefits before their children were born.

During the 1913 strike, the union had issued its members five shilling vouchers, backed by union funds, to enable them to purchase food. It wasn't enough, so they clamored for more, and they found someone at Liberty Hall who couldn't say no to them. When the strike was over, and merchants came to redeem their vouchers, there wasn't enough cash to go around. By 1916, the finger had begun to point to Isaac. He left precipitously for Liverpool, so precipitously that his wife and children had to remain behind. They joined him shortly afterward, and he never returned to Ireland except for brief visits.

Bella, meanwhile, had never fully adjusted to the life of a charwoman, a role for which her upbringing had left her ill-prepared. She fled next door in terror the first time that flour clung to her hands, not realizing that the stuff could easily be washed away. Incongruously, she always wore a pair of spotless white gloves, and neighbors referred to her admiringly as 'Lady Beaver.'

She suffered from headaches which became progressively more frequent and severe, until she had to stop scrubbing floors. The headaches — symptoms of erysipelas — became so painful that she took to wearing a shawl, which made her white gloves appear more incongruous still.

She was wholly dependent on the earnings of her

younger daughter and her two oldest sons, since the youngest boy, John Beaver, wasn't old enough to work, and Susan, incredibly, still wasn't allowed to. Her other daughter, Isabella, was employed as a boxmaker; Valentine Beaver took a job in a coal yard; while 'Sonny' Beaver served briefly as a printer's apprentice and finally joined the navy. Her mother helped her out with occasional gifts of food and clothing, and kindly neighbors donated bread and milk.

The loneliness was as hard to bear as the poverty. Bella saw little of Isaac, or of Tom before he died. Her mother came more often, but the visits must have been difficult. Susan Casey was not a forgiving woman, and she reproached her daughter bitterly for having married against her wishes. Only Mick spent much time with her, keeping her amused with rounds of jokes and stories; but Mick was in the army now. As for O'Casey himself, her contact with him came mainly through her youngest son John, his namesake. O'Casey had taken a liking to the boy, perhaps because, alone of his nieces and nephews, the youngster loved to read. He gave John Beaver the run of his precious library — until one day a book was missing, and O'Casey accused the boy of stealing it. Bella was so angry that she refused to set foot in 18 Abercorn Road until the book was found. (When it finally did turn up, O'Casey hastened to Church Place to apologize — an incident which caused Beaver to remark in later years that his uncle had sunk a foot in his estimation by calling him a thief, and had risen two feet by acknowledging his error.)

The headaches grew worse. On New Year's Day, 1918, Bella shook Valentine Beaver awake and prepared breakfast for him before he went off to work. Afterward she returned to bed, and never awoke. Her death, at the age of 52, was attributed to influenza.

O'Casey has given us an accurate description of her burial Griffin made the funeral arrangements, while O'Casey signed the burial certificate. The Caseys by then were so poor that they couldn't even afford the usual two-horse coach. A lone carriage, drawn by a single horse, followed the hearse to its final resting place at Mt. Jerome.

In September, 1918, Mick received a medical discharge. He'd had an arthritic condition in his right hand before he'd re-entered the service, and his duties as telegraphist had aggravated it. His commanding officer gave him a letter of recommendation, extolling, of all things, his sobriety. With this testimonial in his pocket he had came home and was drinking more than ever. He worked at odd jobs here and there. Paddy McDonnell once ran across him in a streetcleaners outfit, sweeping the gutters for the Dublin corporation.

On November 9, Susan Casey died. Her burial papers record that she was 85. That is probably too old, but she must have been in her early eighties. She'd remained active almost until the end, a familiar little figure in a black bonnet. However, she failed rapidly as death approached, and was bedridden for the last few months of her life.

There is little point in lingering over the death-bed, especially since surviving relatives differ over precisely what occurred. But one thing is clear: events cannot possibly have transpired as O'Casey described them in the moving chapter, *Mrs. Casside Takes a Holiday*. In the first place, he was not alone with her when she died. In the second place, he did not bury her without assistance. His name appears on the burial certificate (he still signed himself Sean O Cathasaigh), but arrangements for the funeral — which took place three days later — were made by an M Casey. This could not possibly have been anyone other than Mick.

So Mick was there, and so was former Volunteer Joe Adams, an old friend of O'Casey's who sat up with him the night after his mother's death. O'Casey, his niece remembers, was profoundly affected, and spent most of the night crying. At one point he rose, draped a red cloth over a little table, set flowers on it, and placed the table next to the coffin, which was lying in the room.

But others who should have been there were not. Griffin was not, having retired from the ministry because of illness earlier in the year. Neither was Isaac, although he'd been notified by telegram of his mother's passing. It was no fault of his. The Armstice had come only the day before the funeral, and wartime regulations were still in effect, requiring travellers to Ireland to notify the authorities three days before their departure. By the time the three day period had elapsed, Susan Casey was buried. But O'Casey didn't understand why his brother hadn't come. He remarked at the time that he would never forgive him, and he kept his vow. When Isaac himself died thirteen years later, his family priest is said to have written to O'Casey, now famous and living in England, asking him to spare some money for the widow. According to Isaac's son Joseph, O'Casey advised the priest in reply to tell Josie that she should rely more on God and less on him; and he alluded with bitterness to his brother's absence from their mother's graveside.

The Club must have seemed strangely empty during the months following the Easter Rising, with so many O'Tooles interned in British detention camps. Some, however, remained behind: Cahill, whose severe limp had prevented him from participating, and Paddy McDonnell. And there were festive occasions, as when Stephen Synnott was married, and O'Casey was deputized to present the newlyweds with a set of dinner plates on behalf of the Club. 'May you always have something to put on it,' he said.

Club members had long been encouraged to patronize the Abbey Theater, where dramas of Irish interest were presented. It occurred to O'Casey that the O'Tooles could present plays of their own. In 1911 he had organized the O'Tooles Pipers Band; now, in 1917 or early 1918, he put his administrative talents to work once again. The result was a drama society, which put on plays or revues at the Empire Theater — now known as the Olympia — or sometimes at the Irish Club on Parnell Square.

Programs survive, flecked with advertisements from Sinn Fein clubs which were springing up all around the city. One such advertisement announces a Christmas raffle at the Sean Connolly club on Amiens Street; another enjoins readers to purchase Sinn Fein Christmas cards; still a third publicizes the first complete book by O'Casey himself, *The Story of Thomas Ashe*. Written under the name O'Cathasaigh, it recounts the martyrdom of an Irish rebel, a close friend of the author's, who had died of ill-treatment in Dublin's Mountjoy Prison.

O'Casey not only fathered the dramatic society, but was one of its most avid contributors and performers. He composed a ballad, *The Constitutional Movement Must Go On*, in which he ridiculed the gradualism of the Parliamentary Party. It culminated in the refrain:

Gather the Party round, Sinn Feiners scorning;
Let your voices roll across the floor.
The constitutional movement, now take warning,
Must go on, and on, and on, forevermore!

Twice a week for six weeks, he and Mick Smith rehearsed the song together. Rehearsals were pleasant, Smith recalls, for O'Casey was a clever partner, easy to work with. On opening night, the two ambled onto the stage, dressed in top hats, frock coats, and boots, and sang before a well-filled house, open to the public but packed largely with friends of the O'Tooles.

He scored his greatest triumph as star of *Nabocklish!*, a comedy about a fatuous English tourist who wants to meet the Irish secret service. His hosts oblige by rigging up a phony one. Their cell holds meetings at which members talk darkly of their murdered victims; but the names of the deceased are really the names of Irish towns and counties: Kill-dare, Kill-kenny. The password, they advise him, is a cut-throat gesture of the hand accompanied by the word *Nabocklish!* (Na bac leis), which is Irish for 'never mind' or 'don't be bothering.' O'Casey took his role as the English tourist so seriously that during rehearsals he arranged to have an English-born lad speak the lines so that he could acquire the proper accent.

Sometime in 1918, Paddy McDonnell invited a young girl named May Keating, who lived on First Avenue just around the corner from the club's Seville Place headquarters, to take part in one of the plays. Thenceforward O'Casey no longer took long walks with McDonnell, but strolled with the young woman instead. This was the 'Maura' of the autobiographies: a plain but vivacious Catholic girl, daughter of a retired police officer who detested O'Casey and tried to dissuade his daughter from seeing him. Opposition came also from another quarter. Parish priest Canon Brady was a good friend of O'Casey's, and had even striven for a time to convert him, only to have him recite from the Koran in reply. But Brady, naturally enough, was opposed to intermarriage, and his voice was joined to that of her father. The combined pressures were too much for her. She and O'Casey stopped seeing one another in 1920 or 1921.

After 1918, O'Casey began by degrees to drop

away from the club. There was no sudden rift this time. It was just that the older generation of O'Tooles was giving way to a new one, and O'Casey found himself increasingly an outsider. It wasn't only that the neophytes were so much younger than he. The Easter Rising was a watershed in Irish history, and there were major differences between the young men who came to maturity before and after it. The pre-1916 generation had been romantic, chivalrous, and innocent. Those who followed were hard-nosed professional gunmen, guerillas in a deadly underground war. They were not interested, as their predecessors had been, in Irish music or Irish plays or Irish pageants. O'Casey treated them with contempt, often interrupting them when they spoke, only to be rebuked by Cahill, who insisted that he listen patiently and wait his turn. 'What are they fighting for Ireland for,' he snarled once, 'when they can't even speak their own language?' The youngsters in turn paid little attention to him, and some of the fanatics among them suspected his loyalty.

He was even quarrelling with Cahill. The Protestant ex-laborer and the Catholic schoolteacher had had their differences in the past without disruption to their friendship. When O'Casey persisted too long on a particularly tender subject, Cahill would try tactfully to shift the conversation to some other issue. He was set in his ways, the schoolmaster once remarked gently, and it would do O'Casey no good to try to change him. 'Listen here, Frank,' came the snappy rejoinder. 'I think any man has a right to change his opinion if he wants to.' Now, however,

81

their disputes became more bitter. O'Casey was wont to heap violent abuse on his enemies. Cahill, the milder of the two, frequently demurred. In particular he reproached O'Casey for his ingratitude to Mick, who was supporting him, and even to Rev. Griffin, who in his quiet way had helped the family with occasional charities. When O'Casey displayed impatience with the youngsters in the club, Cahill sided with his boys.

The ties of their friendship, and the fragile links which still bound O'Casey to the club, were further loosened when he submitted a play, in which the central figure was obviously Cahill. Its title was *The Frost on the Flower*, and, in the script — which has since been lost — O'Casey satirized the schoolmaster for his indecision and failure to make anything of himself. Cahill was deeply wounded. The O'Tooles, in deference to his feelings, rejected the play. Now it was O'Casey's turn to feel aggrieved. The incident rankled on all sides.

Mick had received a partial disability pension of twelve shillings a week in the summer of 1920, and had augmented it from time to time by undertaking various menial jobs. Their nephew John Beaver had lived with them for a while, with O'Casey acting as his guardian — an assignment which he discharged satisfactorily, except that Beaver later complained that his uncle never let him into the street to play, insisting instead that he stay home and read. But eventually Beaver went to live with his sister Susan, now married, leaving Mick and O'Casey alone.

The two brothers had much in common. Both were bright, both were creative, both were contentious. Relatives still insist that Mick was 'the real brains of the family.' Neighbors and drinking companions exclaim admiringly that he had 'words at will,' by which they mean that he was a fluent and witty conversationalist, never at a loss for a snappy rejoinder. Until the end of his life, his speech and writing betrayed the traces of his early education. While both men had a gift for drawing, Mick was by far the more talented artist.

To O'Casey, it must have seemed that Mick put his cleverness to use only in finding new ways to torment him. They'd never gotten along, though an uneasy peace had prevailed between them while their mother was alive. Mick would come home, hatless and coatless (he'd pawned them) and wave a glass of stout under O'Casey's face, growling 'Here, this'll make a man out of you.' He was impervious to his brother's plaintive 'Leave me alone, can't you?' In addition, he had a penchant for coarse practical jokes. In later years, he would substitute a dead cat for a turkey which a neighbor had won in a raffle. Often these jokes were aimed at O'Casey. There was the incident with the bagpipes, which has already been recorded; another time, it is said, Mick gave the police his brother's name instead of his own when he was arrested for disorderly conduct, and O'Casey spent a night in a cell in consequence.

O'Casey cannot be exonerated of all blame for their differences. For many years now, Mick had been bringing in income and O'Casey hadn't — a state of affairs which both men must have resented.

Now their mother's peacekeeping influence was gone, and Mrs. Cunningham in the downstairs front couldn't sleep for the noise of their quarrels. Late one night in the winter of 1920, O'Casey left the flat for the last time and set out for Mountjoy Square, where his old union comrade Mick Mullen lived. He must have proceeded cautiously. Curfew had descended upon a city at war, and many Fluther Goods, many Joxer Dalys were emerging unsteadily from pubs and stumbling over one another in their haste to reach home. The fourth horseman was loose in the land, riding the backs of sullen tanks and closed lorries. Irishmen had come to know that horseman well, and O'Casey knew him better than most, for in earlier days he'd ridden beside him. Now he was leaving the world of John Casey and Sean O Cathasaigh, labor agitator and nationalist. In the new world which he entered that night, he is sufficiently well known, and we need not accompany him further.

Readers familiar with the autobiographies may be curious to learn the fate of the various characters. Pug-faced, pleasant-hearted Georgie Middleton married Frances Maria Harrison, who lived next door to him on St. Mary's Road. He worked as a range setter and died, from the effects of an accident, in 1927 when he was 47 years old. His ancestors had been Presbyterians. The year before his death, he decided that the Church of Ireland had become too romanized, and he reverted to the sterner faith of his fathers.

Harry Fletcher went from St. Barnabas to a London parish. Then, toward the end of his life, he was reassigned to an Irish pulpit, at Stradbury, in the diocese of Killaloe. He died in 1949.

Griffin's health was already broken when he retired from the ministry in 1918. He died, an invalid, in 1923, on the eve of O'Casey's debut as a playwright. His daughter Jenny, who had once made the young O'Casey's heart flutter faster, died in 1923.

Schoolmaster Hogan taught at St. Barnabas until 1909, and is said to have died not long afterward, having taken to drinking heavily in his later years. His daughter succeeded him. Toward the end of his tenure, he caned young Valentine Beaver so severely that Bella came to school to complain.

St. Barnabas itself was closed in March, 1965. The school had ceased its operations eighteen years earlier. Much of the surrounding neighborhood, including 18 Abercorn Road, is said to be marked for demolition. Other O'Casey landmarks are gone already: 85 Dorset Street, where he was born; 35 Mountjoy Square, where he lived during the 1920s. But 9 Innisfallen Parade and 25 Hawthorne Terrace still stand. So do most of the houses where Bella, Isaac, and Tom lived, as well as St. Mary's school which O'Casey attended as a boy (it is owned by a Catholic order now); St. Mary's Church where he was baptized; and the O'Toole's clubhouse on Seville Place, where they moved shortly before O'Casey left them.

Isaac, or Joseph, held several jobs in Liverpool, settling down finally as a foreman in a factory which manufactured auto parts. He remained a strong labor sympathizer. Though bent nearly double by painful ulcers, he walked seven miles to work during the general strike of 1926 rather than take a scab tram. He never saw O'Casey after 1917, though he is said to have attended and enjoyed his brother's plays. He died in 1931, aged 58.

That leaves Mick. Shortly after his brother left him, he gave up his second-story flat at 18 Abercorn Road and moved into the back room downstairs, where he remained until 1939. If he ever saw O'Casey again, the fact is not recorded. Once, accosting Stephen Synnott, he asked, 'Do you ever hear anything of that blind so-and-so brother of mine?' He found work where he could, driving cattle, walking dogs, or drafting letters for neighbors who wanted pensions or other favors from the government.

For two decades he was a familiar sight in the streets and pubs of the North Wall area: a comic little figure in a cap and muffler, with a strutting gait and a walking stick which he carried like a field marshal's baton. His neighbors, who saw no malice in his humor, delight in talking about him, although one suspects that some of their stories are embroidered, for Mick has become something of a legend. His fellow-workers at the cattleyards, who bear such colorful names as Rabbit Kelly, Pitiful Duffy, and Fooker Brown held him in awe, marvelling that a man of breeding and education would match them pint for pint. Even in old age he would sit in one of the North Wall pubs—(usually Nick Welch's—it is Campion's today)—sketching customers and presenting them afterward with their completed portraits.

In 1939, he went to Beaumont to live with Bella's younger daughter, beside the hurling field where O'Casey had played as a young man. There he spent his time reading, or walking, or arguing with priests from the Catholic church nearby. He read the autobiographies avidly. 'The other fella,' he called O'Casey. 'You have to hand it to him.'

The other fella didn't forget him. From time to time Mick would receive mail with an English postmark, and inside there would be a letter and a pound note. 'Here's another quid that may be of some use to you,' O'Casey would write; or 'Enclosed will get you some tobacco for Christmas.' O'Casey knew better. 'Tobacco, says Sean,' said Mick. 'To hell with Sean. We'll blow it.' And blow it he did, drinking a toast to the other fella as he gratefully swallowed the whiskey. Toward the end of his life he grew a Van Dyke beard, and sent a photograph to his brother. O'Casey wrote back, 'You look very venerable — like George Bernard Shaw.' Henceforward the family called him G.B. He died, from a stroke, on January 11, 1947, eleven days after he'd celebrated his 81st birthday.

F.C.